CREATING SWEET DREAMS

CREATING SWEET DREAMS

Rachelle Gershkovich

ISBN: 1522968059
ISBN 13: 9781522968054
Library of Congress Control Number: 2015921431
CreateSpace Independent Publishing Platform
North Charleston, South Carolina

TO MY LOVED ONES

To have a passion and a purpose in this world is a blessing, but to have a support team is priceless. I have been lucky enough to be challenged by the peers in my field to be pushed to be better every day. I would love to thank every person that helped pave this road for me and a little extra thank you to those below.

Thank you Alicen for the endless hours and dedication you gave to this book. You are a beautiful soul and will bring so much to this world. I am not sure I will ever meet a wittier and stronger woman than you.

My sweet Vadim thank you for being my rock, I have never been more loved and supported in all of my life. Thank you from the bottom of my heart!!

The fabulous four, sweet babies of mine, you are my grounding in this beautiful crazy world.

Mom, *What Do You Do with an Idea?* Thank you for helping me see my potential and giving me your blessing along the way.

To my siblings, thank you for the encouragement and mentorship. You have helped guide me in so many ways. Every one of you has held my hand through my highs and lows.

CONTENTS

INTRODUCTION

WHAT MAKES THIS METHOD DIFFERENT AND MORE EFFECTIVE?

CREATING SWEET DREAMS is written based on the method I developed called Baby Created Sleep. It is a gentle, nutrition-based method that focuses on weight, age, and milestones that are developmentally appropriate. I am trying to break the trend of people stating, "My baby is a certain age, so he should sleep this much." My method has proven effective and allows babies to determine when they are developmentally ready to move to the next stage of sleep. We opt to work with babies' bodies, metabolisms, and sleep cycles so that they learn how to sleep through the night with positive and healthy associations.

Rather than attempting to train your baby's behavior, you will focus on reading your baby's signals of readiness for the next transition. Baby Created Sleep consists of four transitions to guide you through elongating the nighttime stretches of sleep. It brings forth a method that is far more effective and healthy for your baby's development as well as your mental well-being. I am taking the "training" out of sleep training, and instead I am focusing on supporting and guiding your baby through the natural progression of sleep. Below is an overview of the gradual increase in nighttime sleep that will support your baby's body.

Eight pounds	One four-hour stretch in a twenty-four-hour period
Ten pounds	One four- to six-hour stretch in a twenty-four-hour period
Twelve pounds	One six- to eight-hour stretch in a twenty-four-hour period
Fifteen pounds	One ten-hour stretch in a twenty-four-hour period

HOW TO READ THIS BOOK

You can read this book in a couple of different ways. The first option would be to read it cover to cover and then reference each transition as your little one is ready. Another option would be to just read the section that applies to where you are currently at. Our final option is for the sleep-deprived parent. Each section has titles that are bolded and paragraphs that are italicized. This is the important takeaway information that will help you to sleep train your little one without reading the entire book.

However you decide to read this book, know that it can be kept and used as a reference, both for your first child as well as any children to come. The methods and practices are detailed enough to be helpful, but also take into consideration that children grow and develop at their own pace.

DISCLAIMER

This book, while based solely on evidence-based research and information, is not a medical book. The advice is simply that great advice that has been used successfully by many and designed to help parents succeed in sleep training their children.

ABOUT THE AUTHOR

I am a married mother of four, and I love my children more than anything in the world. I work hard to provide them a life that is full of love, support, and everything they could possibly need. Long before I had children, I was interested in childcare and childhood development. As the second youngest of five children of a widow, I grew up in Colorado taking care of my younger brother. I would describe him as being "my baby" and credit this for the start of my interest in caring for young babies for a living.

It wasn't until 2002 that I began what was to become my lifelong career in sleep training and night-nanny work. This work, coupled with several nursing and nutrition classes, led me to realize that nutrition is key in the development of a child, and it helped fuel my desire for this career. I then decided to attend Metropolitan State University of Denver, majoring in human nutrition and dietetics. I studied how nutrition affects the body and how it can be manipulated to help the body thrive.

While starting the sleep-training process with my second daughter, I realized much of the advice I received from family, friends, or books went against my natural instincts. Additionally, many of the techniques I tried didn't seem to actually work. I tried to implement one of the most traditional and popular methods of sleep training. It not only did not work at all but in fact seemed to cause additional problems. On top of that, the process made me feel awful. The method suggested techniques such as behavioral training, time crying, self-soothing, and unrealistic scheduling that did not coincide with my baby. So I began to look for alternatives.

After struggling for weeks with this and other ineffective methods of sleep training, I wondered what would happen if I incorporated sleep training into my baby's metabolism that I was currently studying. I was curious how the two systems of metabolism and sleep cycles would affect each other. Rather than working with behavior, as with the current method, I wiped the slate and focused solely on my daughter's current abilities with her caloric intake, stomach size, sleep cycles, and motor skills. I took extra care to give her all the calories she needed during a twenty-four-hour period in the daytime and to not give her calories at night.

What happened next was like magic. As soon as I started working with her metabolism instead of her behavior, sleeping through the night became a matter of time, and the initial effects were almost immediate. My daughter was happy and sleeping great, and I knew this was the right way to support her.

I ran with this newfound discovery. I knew I had stumbled on something that went much further than luck or that just applied to my own child. I had found a new way to both care for and sleep train a baby that would change the field itself. This discovery into the science of a baby's sleep and growth eventually resonated with all the people it touched.

Now I have established a solid, proven, and effective method of caring for and sleep training babies, which I teach to others at the Infant Institute. In 2010, I founded a night-nanny agency, Maternal Instincts, where we focus on teaching and supporting parents with postpartum care and sleep training in their homes.

Baby Created Sleep is a method of sleep training and care that is not only developmentally appropriate but works with a baby's biological functions. While creating the method itself, I worked with science, childhood development, motor-skill development, emotional development, caloric intake, mother intuition, and my previous experience with sleep support to devise a system that would be not only effective but nurturing.

I continue working with families in their homes to support sleep because I am passionate about Baby Created Sleep. I still love working hands-on with families, as each new family and each new baby brings more insight to my amazement of these little humans and their capabilities. It is an honor to have helped hundreds of families and their babies create sweet dreams.

TOOLS FOR SLEEP TRAINING

HERE ARE SOME tips that will prepare your little one for sleep training once they are ready. You can also use this as a resource to refer back to throughout each transition, if you have any questions.

YOUR BABY'S HUNGER CUES

Understanding your baby's hunger cues is beneficial as food is crucial to health, growth, and development. A hungry baby will likely tell you in several specific ways that he or she is hungry. These are the cues to be aware of and to look for:

1. Opening mouth
2. Smacking or licking lips
3. Rooting side to side
4. Sucking on hands
5. Aggravated movement
6. Crying

A great way to tell if your baby is full is by the way the arm is positioned. If the arm is up, then baby is still hungry. If his or her arm is down and resting by the side, then baby is full. Think of it as the opposite of a tank of gas; when the arm goes down, the tank is full. This method works for both bottle and breastfed babies; however, if you are breastfeeding, you may want to pay closer attention to this, as you don't usually measure your breast milk, and it is, therefore, important to listen to your baby's cues.

WHEN TO FEED YOUR BABY FOR THE FIRST EIGHT WEEKS

It is important to know and understand how quickly babies grow and how the caloric intake they need at various ages changes, especially when it comes to sleep training as weight gain and nutrition are central to the Baby Created Sleep method. From days one to three, a breastfed baby's source of nutrients is colostrum, which protects your baby's digestive tract and builds the immune system. Only about five to seven milliliters of colostrum are produced per feed, which makes it normal for baby to feed every hour. It is important to never let your baby go more than three hours between feeds.

The more skin-to-skin contact you have with your baby, the more quickly your milk production initiates. Starting on day four, feed your baby on demand every two to three hours. You're looking at eight to twelve feeds in a twenty-four-hour period. After week three, your baby will be eating an average of twenty-five ounces a day. A breastfed baby will take in anywhere from two to four ounces per feed. With a formula-fed baby, you still want to encourage that range, but don't try to force a full feed if the baby is not interested.

Babies may go through a "witching hour" a few hours each day before bedtime. A "witching hour" is when your baby is fussier than normal but is not hungry, doesn't need to be changed, and isn't helped by soothing. It is not unusual for your baby to want to cluster feed during this time (eat every hour versus every two hours).[1]

BIRTH WEEK THREE (FEEDINGS IN TWENTY-FOUR HOURS)

From the time a baby is born, he or she will be increasing his or her feeds very quickly over the first few weeks. With a bottle, you can see these changes through the amount of ounces they actually consume. After day five, you will want to aim for sixteen to eighteen ounces in the full twenty-four-hour period. This will require a lot of feeds with high frequency. It is not realistic to wait three to four hours for a feed when they are this young. There is no real floor time at this

---

1 Be aware that this "witching hour" is a *huge* indication that your baby needs a nervous-system reset.

age, and any activity can be done on your chest. Below is an overview of what feedings can look like for the first three weeks of your little one's life. Take note that it will rapidly increase from day one to day twenty-one.

Age	Day 1-2	Day3-6	Day7-14	Day15-21
Feeds	5ml-7ml per feed	22ml-27ml	45ml-60ml (1.5-2 oz)	90ml-120ml (3-4 oz)
Frequency of feeds	Every 1-2 hours (10-12 Feeds)	Every 2 hours (10-12 Feeds)	Every 2 hours (10-12 Feeds)	Every 2-3 hours (8 -12 Feeds)
Activity	No floor time	No floor time	No floor time	No floor time
Breast-sleeping	20-23 Hours	20-22 Hours	18-20 Hours	16-20 Hours

Breast sleeping: a term used by Dr. McKenna as a sleep style of which a baby is sleeping at the breast and eating. This is often the type of sleep a baby does in the first few weeks. With bottle feeding, it is ideal to also feed your baby in a breastfeeding position and switch side to side.

Keep in mind that 30 ml equals 1 oz.

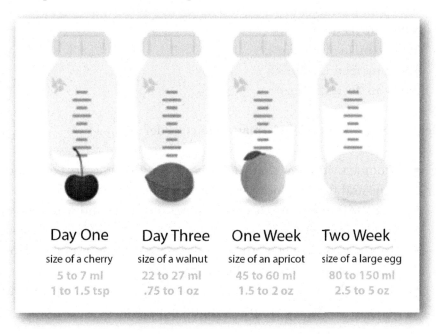

Day One	Day Three	One Week	Two Week
size of a cherry	size of a walnut	size of an apricot	size of a large egg
5 to 7 ml	22 to 27 ml	45 to 60 ml	80 to 150 ml
1 to 1.5 tsp	.75 to 1 oz	1.5 to 2 oz	2.5 to 5 oz

WEEKS THREE TO EIGHT

First, you need to be aware that one ounce of formula equals twenty calories, and one ounce of breast milk equals, on average, twenty-two calories. Once babies are three weeks old, they need to consume five hundred calories a day. If your baby consumes twenty-four ounces of formula in a day, that is only 480 calories, whereas twenty-four ounces of breast milk will equal 528 calories. Therefore, formula-fed babies need to eat more during the day.

Here is a schedule that will help ensure your little one is eating enough calories during the day.

6:00 a.m. feed (2–4 oz.)
8:00 a.m. feed (2–4 oz.)
10:00 a.m. feed (2–4 oz.)
12:00 p.m. feed (2–4 oz.)
2:00 p.m. feed (2–4 oz.)
4:00 p.m. feed (2–4 oz.)
6:00 p.m. feed (2–4 oz.)
8:00 p.m. feed (2–4 oz.)
10:00 p.m. feed (2–4 oz.)
1:00 a.m. feed (2–4 oz.)
4:00 a.m. feed (2–4 oz.)

Here is some additional information to consider:

- Floor activity a few times a day is ideal at this age. Try back floor time and tummy floor time five to ten minutes at a time.
- Naps will be twenty to sixty minutes at a time and will happen five to seven times a day.
- Total ounces will need to be 24–25 oz. with formula at 20 cal/oz. (the normal formula on the shelf).
- The feeds will range 2–4 oz. at each feed. Do not expect your baby to eat the exact same amount at each feed.

Use this chart as a general reference for the first thirty days.

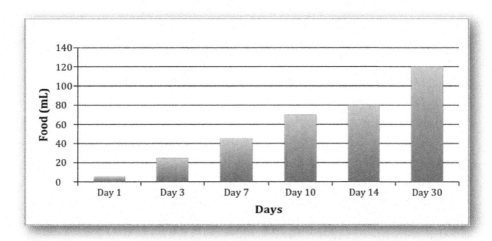

The following table shows the drastic increase of calories as your little one begins to develop over the first year of life. It emphasizes the importance that milk will have on your baby's nutrition and the number of ounces needed to achieve this.

Daily Minimums	Breast Milk	Formula
After 3 weeks, baby needs 500 calories daily	Approximately 22.7 oz.	Approximately 25 oz.
After 6 months, baby needs 650 calories daily	Approximately 100 calories from solid food, and 25 oz. of breast milk	Approximately 100 calories from solid food, and 27.5 oz. of formula
After 9 months, baby need 900 calories	Approximately 200 calories from solid food, and 27-28 oz. of breast milk	Approximately 200 calories from solid food and 30 oz. of formula

DISPELLING MYTHS

DON'T WAKE A SLEEPING BABY.
This is completely false. It is important that babies eat often so that they do not become dehydrated. So if your little one is on a longer stretch of sleep, you will need to wake him or her up to feed.

HOLDING BABIES TOO MUCH MAKES THEM SPOILED.
This is irrelevant for babies under sixteen weeks old. It is important to hold young babies often; they can't be held too much. This myth is really age inappropriate and doesn't come into play for a long time.

DON'T FEED BABIES TOO MUCH, OR THEY WILL BECOME FAT.
This is false. As long as you make sure you stay within the range of calories they need for a day, they will be just fine.

CRYING IS GOOD FOR A BABY'S LUNGS.
False! All extended crying does is burn calories. This can be potentially harmful if they do it too much. Also, crying is the only form of communication babies have at this age. A crying baby is trying to tell you something.

A few additional things about infant care to note:

- All babies experience a gassy stage while they are building their digestive systems. It will peak between three and nine weeks. This often causes restlessness, and your baby is typically noisy (grunting).
- When they come home, all babies have a form of reflux because their sphincters are not fully closed. This phase is typically during the first six to eight weeks. If your baby fails to thrive or experiences severe pain, seek help from your pediatrician. To remedy this, you can take the following actions:
    - Hold baby for an extra fifteen to twenty minutes after each feed to help the food settle.
    - Hold or rest baby at a forty-five-degree angle.
    - Put your hand on the baby's stomach and add a little pressure to help with pains from gas.

BEDTIME

A bedtime routine should be short and sweet. You want this to be easily repeatable and enjoyable for your entire family. Start by telling your baby you are going to bed and talking about sleep in a happy manner. Your baby is never too young to talk to and to set up the night on a happy note. I prefer not to use bath in bedtime routines because it is too long, their skin does not need that much soap, and it's not always calming to babies.

You want this to be a long-term routine, so add in a song and book at a young age. The entire process should be thirty to forty-five minutes and *always* started at the same time each night. With the circadian rhythms being so new, you need to set up a bedtime you can stick to. This sets up your entire night.

TIME LINE OF NORMAL SLEEP

Newborns love to sleep, so expect them to sleep a lot. For the first two weeks, your new baby will sleep anywhere from sixteen to eighteen hours in a twenty-four-hour period (as seen below). It is only in the third week of life that they will begin to transition into sleeping slightly less than this, although still somewhere in the range of sixteen hours in a twenty-four-hour period. You will notice that your baby has "woken up" during the third week, and this will pair with an increased appetite and a growth spurt. After three weeks, your baby's sleep decreases even more, coming down to around twelve to sixteen hours of sleep a day. If your baby is trying to sleep longer than three-hour stretches in the first three weeks, you will want to wake them. It seems counterproductive to wake a sleeping baby, but sleep is not our main focus at this young age—weight gain is.

Then, at around eight weeks, your baby's circadian rhythms begin to come into play, which increases the amount of time spent asleep during the night. Circadian rhythms are developed in three stages: (1) at birth regulating temperature, (2) between six to eight weeks, and (3) between eight to twelve weeks. The total amount of sleep within a twenty-four-hour period will generally decrease to eleven to fourteen hours total and will remain there until your child is around three years of age (this has to do with naps and the loss of them).

Sleep changes significantly at around eight to twelve weeks due to melatonin (a hormone for drowsiness) and cortisol (a hormone for alertness). In utero, your baby was regulated by the mother's hormones and physiological cues. After birth, sleep is based on a survival mode (the homeostatic system), where food intake and digestion are the reasons for waking and sleeping. Babies wake to eat and then sleep to conserve calories and energy during their rapid growth.

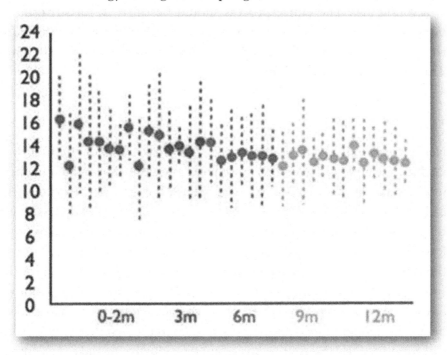

Above is a sleep chart (taken from Infant Sleep Information Source in the United Kingdom) for you to use as a general reference for how much and when you can expect your baby to sleep. However, this chart also shows how much these sleep patterns can vary. The y-axis indicates hours of sleep, and the x-axis represents the child's age. Additionally, the large dots indicate average amount of sleep for the age, while the small dashes indicate the range.

Although your baby seems to be getting a lot of sleep, it is usually random for the first eight weeks and will not be for extended periods of time for the first few months. This means no more eight-hour nights for you, at least not for a while. Therefore, it will be important that you get sleep whenever you can so that you can maintain your energy and continue caring for your new baby. Take a lot of short and sweet naps during the day and night, at the same times your baby does. This may be challenging at first, but it is important for you to get sleep when you can. Also, you might try using friends, family, and hired help so that you can care for yourself and get some sleep as well. If you don't care for yourself to some extent, it will be harder for you to take care of your baby.

FOURTH TRIMESTER

It is important for the mother to not only establish a secure feeding relationship early on with the new baby but also to establish bonding. It is equally as important for nonbirthing parents to get time with their babies early on as well, especially through skin-to-skin contact. This is because spending time with the baby and doing what's called *kangaroo care* really helps the bond grow between parent and baby, and it helps make this baby more "real" (*Kangaroo Care* 2015). This is the foundation for building the communication and understanding you'll need for success in sleep training later.

Kangaroo care is skin-on-skin contact between a baby and a parent. Place the baby, only in a diaper, onto the bare chest of the parent, and cover the baby's back with a blanket. Nonbirthing parents don't get to feel the baby grow inside them for nine months, and they need touch after birth to begin to create a strong bond. Also, during the fourth trimester, your baby will learn who to turn to for nourishment, both physically and emotionally, so it is extremely important that both you and your partner are present during this time.

The first eight weeks are the key to setting up the beginning of sleep training your baby. When these weeks are free of schedules, routines, and chaos, and are instead focused solely on the baby and development of parent-baby bonds, the transition into implementing a schedule and extending nighttime sleep will come much more easily, both for parents and baby. Mastering soothing techniques increases your ability to communicate and understand your baby's needs. This will play a role with each transition through your sleep support.

	8:00 p.m.	9:00 p.m.	10:00 p.m.	11:00 p.m.	12:00 a.m.	1:00 a.m.	2:00 a.m.	3:00 a.m.	4:00 a.m.	5:00 a.m.	6:00 a.m.
Structure	Bedtime (45 minute routine should be completed already)	Progress as normal, feeding baby 4 oz. at each wake in the night (8:00 pm to 6:00 am)									Start off the day with a full 4 oz. feed
Transition One	Bedtime (45 minute routine should be completed already)	If baby wakes, soothe back to sleep (8:00 pm to 12:00 am. This is one 4-hour stretch, without a feed.)			When baby wakes, give 4 oz. feed		When baby wakes, give 4 oz. feed		When baby wakes, give 4 oz. feed		Start off the day with a full 4 oz. feed
Transition Two	Bedtime (45 minute routine should be completed already)	If baby wakes, soothe back to sleep (8:00 pm to 2:00 am. This is one 6-hour stretch, without a feed.)					When baby wakes, give 4 oz. feed		When baby wakes, give 4 oz. feed		Start off the day with a full 4 oz. feed
Transition Three	Bedtime (45 minute routine should be completed already)	If baby wakes, soothe back to sleep (8:00 pm to 4:00 am. This is one 8-hour stretch, without a feed.)							When baby wakes, give 4 oz. feed		Start off the day with a full 4 oz. feed
Transition Four	Bedtime (45 minute routine should be completed already)	If baby wakes, soothe back to sleep (8:00 pm to 4:00 am. This is one 8-hour stretch, without a feed.)							When baby wakes, give 2 oz. feed		Start off the day with a full 4 oz. feed
Solidify Training	Bedtime (45 minute routine should be completed already)	If baby wakes, soothe back to sleep (8:00 pm to 6:00 am.) This is one 10-hour stretch, without a feed. Do this for 2 to 3 weeks to solidify the process.									Start off the day with a full 4 oz. feed

SLEEP POSITIONS

Sleep positions will be an important piece to the puzzle for healthy sleeping. Most babies have been sleeping in a propped position and will now go to a flat surface. This is also the time to decide the sleep space/location since we will base our schedule heavily on the bedtime routine and the associations created with the sleep space. It is ideal to have your baby sleeping in the same space all night long compared to starting in the nursery and moving to the family bed after a few feeds. Instead, review the safe-sleep options below and remain in one sleep space all night long with your baby through the multiple night feeds and wakes.

Most babies prefer to sleep in an upright or forty-five-degree angle for the first eight to twelve weeks. This is a flat surface that is elevated or a sleeping device that is made at an angle. This is okay up until the eight- to twelve-week mark, when your baby needs to transition to sleeping on a flat surface (Coley 2015). Babies can, however, sleep on either their backs, which is the safest sleeping position (Healthychildren.org 2012), or their stomachs.[2] It is only safe for them to sleep on their stomachs once they are fully capable of rolling. This is not typical at eight weeks, so make sure to watch for this during their naps as they should not be stomach sleeping at night at this age.

Cosleeping is also highly recommended for the first twelve months of your baby's life (Healthychildren.org 2012). This means a parent or adult should sleep within arm's reach of baby for the first year. It allows you to keep a close watch on your baby, and it helps to coregulate your baby's systems.

In addition to cosleeping, be aware that it is important to swaddle your baby with hands up in the first three to six weeks. Your baby will give

---

2 It is important to note that it is not safe for babies to sleep on their stomachs until they can get in and out of the position on their own. So babies should never be laid down to sleep on their stomachs, and, if they turn over on their own to sleep on their stomachs, they must be really good at rolling over multiple times (called "barrel rolling") before they are left to sleep like this. Note that becoming good at rolling doesn't usually happen until approximately four to six months of age, so, until then, babies will need to sleep lying on their backs.

you many hunger cues besides crying, and if you swaddle hands down, you will suppress these cues. As the feeding relationship between you and your baby is established, these signs will be better developed, and swaddling hands down will become safe. As soon as your baby can roll over, swaddling is no longer safe. This is because babies are strong and can break out of their blankets and could then get caught up in them.

In summary, here are the main points:

- One to six weeks: swaddle hands up
- Six weeks to four months: swaddle hands down
- Four to six months or when your baby can roll over: don't swaddle

Furthermore, you really need to be aware of the different dangerous sleep positions and locations for babies, which include, but are not limited to, the couch, unsafe bed or crib surfaces, swaddling after your baby can roll, and stomach sleeping for a baby who cannot roll. The couch (or a recliner) is the all-time worst place to take a nap with your baby. This is because there are so many crevices your baby could roll or fall into and then suffocate. Make sure to avoid dangerous sleeping positions as they are not worth the risk.

BED-SHARING AND CRIB-SLEEPING TIPS

If your baby is going to sleep in the bed with you, then it is important that you adhere completely to the following guidelines for your child's safety: no smoking by either parent; no drug or alcohol use of any kind, not even prescription drugs; and no loose blankets. Ideally, your bed is low to the ground, and you will not let yourself get overtired. Neither parent can be obese. In addition, your baby must be breastfed. This is because breastfed babies will learn to roll toward the source of food (i.e., breast) and will roll in the direction of the mother. However, bottle-fed babies don't know where their food source comes from. For more information on safe bed sharing and "breast sleeping," please refer to Dr. James McKenna's work at Naturalchild.org.

As far as crib sleeping goes, there are guidelines you should follow as well. First, the temperature in the room where the crib is should be between sixty-nine and seventy-two degrees Fahrenheit. Babies cannot have any sort of blanket in the crib while they sleep. You also need to make sure that your baby is warm enough, hence the need for a warm/consistent temperature. Also there should be no toys or bumper pads in the crib while baby is sleeping. Bumpers and blankets can be introduced to the sleep space once the baby is rolling and is no longer swaddled.

Finally, even if your baby sleeps in a crib and you opt to not cosleep, baby should sleep in the parents' bedroom for six to twelve months according to the American Academy of Pediatrics. I recommend getting to an eight-hour stretch before moving your baby to his or her own room to help you with night feeds not interrupting your sleep as much as walking down the hall to your baby's room.

SOOTHING TECHNIQUES—THE FIVE S'S AND MORE

There are many great tools you can use to soothe a baby. Sometimes one method may work while another does not. This can vary depending on what time of day it is, what has upset your baby, who is doing the soothing, and even just your baby's personal preference. Therefore, it will be beneficial to you to be versed in multiple styles. The most common types of soothing are known as "the five Ss." These are swaddle, sound, suction, swatting, and side or stomach positioning.

Swaddling can happen in two ways: arms up and arms down. Let's start with swaddling with arms up.

1. Choose your swaddle blanket—it can be a normal baby blanket or an actual blanket designed for swaddling.
2. Spread it out and lay your baby in the center.
3. Tuck your baby's arms up close to the chin, with the arms either slightly over the chest or by the side (with hands still tucked up to chin), and bring one side of the blanket over and across your baby's arms, tucking tightly underneath the body.

4. Bring the other side of the blanket over and across your baby, bringing it all the way around the back, and tuck down into the top of the blanket to secure.

5. Make sure that you wrap at shoulder height so that your baby's mouth can reach the fists.

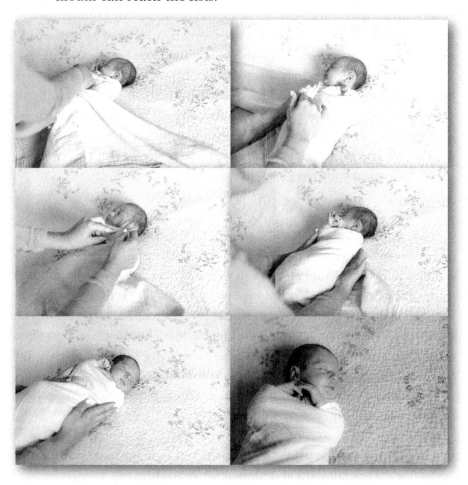

When you are finished swaddling, the tightest part of the swaddle should be around the middle, and the loosest part should be around the feet. This allows your baby to practice motor skills by moving and kicking feet without restriction and without breaking free of the swaddle. This technique is used for very young babies as it allows them to show their hunger cues.

Now, let's talk about swaddling with the arms down.

1. Choose your blanket, and lay it down on a flat surface so that it is angled in the shape of a diamond.
2. Take one of the corners, and fold it down about eight inches toward the center.
3. Lay your baby onto the blanket so that his or her shoulders line up with the flat edge you have just created.
4. Put your baby's left arm straight down next to baby's side. Bring that side of the blanket over and across your baby's abdomen and arm, and tuck it in tightly under the back.
5. Place your baby's right arm down by the side. Bring the remaining corner of the blanket over and across your baby's abdomen and arm, and then wrap around the back and tuck into the top of the blanket to secure.

Remember that while swaddling is a great tool to use to soothe your baby, it should not be used during the daytime. Swaddling suppresses your baby's cues and movements. Instead, only use it to help suppress involuntary movements during the night so that your baby can rest without being woken by his or her natural reflexes. See below for the step-by-step process for swaddling with the arms down.

Sound can mean multiple things. It can mean holding your baby to your chest and humming lightly, and it can also mean making soft "sh" noises. Depending on your home (if it's a louder environment with other kids), it can even mean placing a sound machine in your baby's room at night. This sound helps drown out other voices and noises in your home that may make it more difficult for your baby to fall and stay asleep. It can also help to serve as a constant for your baby throughout all the sleep cycles.

If you opt for this, the sound *must* remain constant. Don't set a timer so that the sound machine turns off after a certain number of minutes, otherwise this will disrupt your baby's sleep cycles. The sound must remain constant all night long and be a genuine white noise. Additionally, the sound machine can't have a nightlight as any light (except red) will disrupt the baby's circadian rhythms.

Suction is an extremely effective soothing tool. Your little one has many reflexes around his or her mouth, cheeks, and nose. Satisfying these reflexes is very comforting for him or her. Use it as a tool, and like any one of these tools, use it only as needed. Be aware that a pacifier can suppress hunger cues; being in tune with your baby's hunger cues will help to eliminate this as an issue.

Swatting is essentially patting your baby lightly on the bum, belly, or back, sometimes accompanied by a sort of rocking motion. This works well if your baby wakes and needs to be soothed as it calms him or her without having to lift your baby in your arms.

Side- or stomach-laying positions relieve the Moro reflex. This is normally present in newborns for up to three to five months after birth. "It is a response to a sudden loss of support or loud sound, which then makes the infant become extremely startled and/or feel as if they are falling" (Cherry 2015). It is also just a comfortable position for your baby. Make sure that after soothing, you must turn your baby onto his or her back. You can't leave babies on their sides because they may roll over onto their stomachs, and if they aren't capable of barrel rolling when they do this, you have to roll them back yourself. You can also use side soothing in your arms or stomach soothing on your chest as you lay back. For a reflux baby, this can be helpful with the pain, and for all babies, a mama's or papa's chest is a great place to rest.

Secure touch is useful when you place a hand on your baby's stomach and add slight pressure. Then slowly pull your hand away, hovering about half an inch away from your baby's stomach before pulling away completely. Don't make any sudden movements as this can startle your baby.

Bum rocking is when you place your baby to his or her side or stomach and put your hand on his or her bum and rock baby's body back and forth gently. Do this until your baby calms, and then stop the rocking but keep your hand placed firm on baby's bottom. After a short time, slowly pull your hand away.

Laying your baby down is often a point of stress for parents and is ideal to work on from day one. Be aware of the proper way to lay your baby down so as not to trigger the Moro reflex. This is often referred to as the startle reflex, where your baby's arms will flail out, and they look scared.

Keeping your baby close to you and moving your body with your baby toward the sleep surface will help eliminate triggering the Moro reflex. Lay your baby down with your body touching the baby's, chest to chest, and remain over your baby. Hover for a moment or until you feel your baby's body relax. Then, replace your body with your hand to continue the pressure and security on his or her chest. When you pull away, do so slowly. Do not simply use your arms to lay your baby down, or baby will feel as though falling and jerk awake.

COREGULATING YOUR INFANT'S SYSTEMS

NERVOUS SYSTEM

Babies' nervous systems take up to three years to develop enough for them to be able to reset them on their own (*Zero to Three* 2014). Therefore, babies will need help to reset their systems for the first three years of their lives. Resetting your baby's nervous system will be one of the most important parts of your job as a parent. This is because it is the system babies have the least control of and the system that parents have the most control helping with.

You can really change your baby's mood and demeanor by resetting the nervous system, which will, in turn, make both you and your baby's lives easier. To reset the nervous system, bring your baby to your chest, put a hand flat on his or her head, and engage in deep breathing. It is important that you do not make any noise and do not move. Focus all your energy on remaining calm and concentrate on the stillness and breathing of both you and your baby. Your sense of calm and controlled breathing will coregulate your baby's system and bring him or her back to calm.

Your baby's nervous system needs to be reset multiple times through the day. Cortisol levels build up (i.e., the hormone in the body that signals stress), and your baby will become overstimulated. The system will eventually reset by accident or without you being aware that resetting has occurred. This usually happens when you are both crying at the same time while you hold your baby to your chest. Or it could happen while you are breastfeeding your baby. The more aware of it you are and the more often you do it, the more in control of the situation you will be, and the happier and more agreeable your baby will be.

Mothers and their babies are in sync with each other, and so your (i.e., Mom's) presence is often calming. When you are gone and your baby is left to cry, both you and your baby's cortisol levels increase. The difference between you and your baby is that while your nervous system will reset on its own, and your cortisol levels will decrease and regulate, your baby's won't (Middlemiss et al. 2011). Even though babies may stop crying, (because they've cried themselves out), their cortisol levels will remain high. This is a problem because it results in mothers' and babies' systems being out of sync with each other, creating a negative association to the sleep space and a lack of communication with each other.

You will often use a combination of the above-mentioned techniques and also create some of your own. Each relationship created with a baby is different, and what works for Mom may not work for a partner, grandparent, caregiver, and so forth. When working through sleep transitions, you will use the soothing techniques you know work best first and slowly wean to the least invasive one—ideally, just a calming touch.

DIGESTIVE SYSTEM

This system will be developing for the first year of life with multiple different transitions. Babies' digestive systems actually start working in the womb, helping them digest the nutrients they get from their mothers. Strangely enough, babies don't usually have their first bowel movements until the first or second day after they are born (except with late babies, who likely expel *meconium* when they are born).[3]

The development of the digestive system involves a stage when your baby will be exceptionally gassy. This period will be most intense from weeks three through nine and occurs, in part, because the digestive system is maturing and the immune system is increasing through the babies' digestive tracts as they process Mom's milk. The colostrum, which is your baby's first food, will line your infant's digestive tract and begin building the immune system. Additionally, babies don't have much core strength, and so they actually have to work at passing gas, which can be a painful and frustrating experience for them. A tip for helping your baby through this is to place your baby on your chest for fifteen to twenty minutes after a feeding, which will both aid in digestion and reduce reflux.

Milk that is introduced to your baby's digestive tract will affect the pH balance in the system and support development in this fragile digestive system. Every time your baby is exposed to a new food for the first year, you are helping to build and support development in the digestive system. For the first six months, your baby will depend on the lipids in

3 "The first fecal excretion of a newborn child [is] composed chiefly of bile, mucus, and epithelial cells" (Dictionary.com 2016).

milk to support rapid growth. Once you add in solids, the development continues as they expose baby's stomach to the complex and dynamic structure of food for the human body.

pH SYSTEM

It will take up to ten days for your baby's *pH system* to regulate in your baby's digestive tract.[4] So, for example, every time you introduce a new food, it will take ten days for the baby's pH to regulate. Therefore, if you switch formulas, give it two weeks to see the results—unless you see blood in the stool, which is an indicator of a whey protein allergy or intolerance (Mayo Clinic Staff 2014). You can tell that the pH system has regulated when things like constipation or diarrhea become more normal. Finally, be aware that any medication that is given to your baby takes two weeks to start seeing results. This is simply protocol.

Everything we have discussed up to this point has filled your tool belt. You can pick and choose which tools will be most beneficial as you support your little one through longer stretches of sleep at night. As baby rapidly grows and develops over the course of the first year, these tools can be used in many different variations through many different stages. As we begin this process, make sure to remember the tools you've learned.

---

4 Note that the pH system is one of the most important biochemical balances in all human body chemistry and controls the speed of the body's biochemical reactions. "It stands for the measurement of the hydrogen ion concentration in the body" (Felicetti 2012).

TRANSITION ONE

―――――――⌒――――――――

EIGHT WEEKS, EIGHT POUNDS: SEPARATING DAY FROM NIGHT

YOUR BABY HAS completed the fourth trimester and has had some time adjusting to his or her new environment. It is now time to begin differentiating your baby's days from nights and working with his or her newly developed circadian rhythms for nighttime sleep. This is a very exciting time for parents to transition out of the twenty-four-hour schedule into a twelve-hour schedule (separating day/night). In order to work through this transition, we will go over the schedule, plan, and details for implementing healthy sleep associations and ways to work with your baby's body to support healthy sleep.

At this point, your baby is now eight weeks old, and you've been to the pediatrician for your checkup. I want you to follow your baby's growth chart and make sure that he or she stays within 10 percent of his or her previous percentile at each checkup to show consistent growth. Your baby will have increased his or her amount of eating to around twenty-four ounces per day of formula or breast milk and be a much more efficient eater. If you are feeding with bottles, you can try to increase the stage nipple you are using to increase flow. With breastfeeding, you should notice your baby can eat more milk, more quickly and feel satisfied after each feed.

Circadian rhythms, you may have noticed, are starting to show up at this time. The easiest way to know this is that your baby will no longer be pooping at nighttime. Also, your baby will be more alert during the day and show signs of sleepiness as the sun sets. It will also be easier to get your baby back to sleep quickly when feeding throughout the night (as long as no lights are turned on).

It is possible your baby is taking a large daytime nap that pushes a feed to four hours. At this time, we will be switching that longer daytime stretch to the nighttime sleep and reserve the day for high activity, food intake, and stimulation.

DEVELOPMENTAL PROGRESSION

Your baby's development will vary at this age, but you will begin to see his or her personality evolve. With eye contact, smiling, and laughing, you will enjoy the days spent getting to know your little one. It is also a good time to learn your baby's cries and forms of communicating with you to aid in your ability to meet his or her needs.

At two months, your baby should do the following:

- Smile at people
- Begin to calm himself or herself in stressful situations (if only very briefly)
- Attempt to make eye contact
- Pay attention to and recognize certain people's faces
- Make "cooing" and "gooing" sounds
- Responding to (turning his or her head toward) sounds he or she doesn't make himself or herself
- Begin to show signs of boredom if activities don't change often enough
- Hold his or her head up
- Push up a bit with his or her arms when lying on his or her stomach
- Begin to have more fluid and deliberate movements

Warning signs at two months:

- Doesn't respond to loud sounds
- Doesn't watch things move in his or her immediate surroundings

- Doesn't smile at people
- Doesn't bring his or her hands to his or her mouth
- Can't hold his or her head up or push up a bit on his or her arms

SLEEP TRAINING YOUR BABY

Is your baby ready for a four-hour stretch? Check all boxes that apply.

- ☐ My baby is eight pounds.
- ☐ My baby is at least eight weeks.
- ☐ I've completed the eight-week checkup with my pediatrician, and he feels the baby is ready for a longer stretch of sleep.
- ☐ My baby's circadian rhythms have come into play.
- ☐ My baby is *not* sick.
- ☐ My baby has not had any vaccinations within the last forty-eight hours.

If you have checked all of these boxes, then you are ready to start sleep training! The first step is creating a strong nighttime routine and a feeding schedule throughout the day to ensure your little one is getting enough calories to push for longer stretches without feeds at nighttime. Use the following information to help build routines for both the morning and night.

CREATING A DAYTIME SCHEDULE

A strong daytime schedule will include playtimes, nap times, and a feeding schedule (remembering to make sure calories are appropriate for growth spurts that happen). It is important to keep this routine as consistent yet accommodating to your baby as possible. Although it may not always be feasible to maintain an exact schedule every day, it should be as similar as possible each day. For some families, a schedule is helpful and a safe guide to follow, but for other families, it's not a good fit. Don't force a schedule if it is not a current lifestyle choice. Instead, adhere to the most important parts as bullet points or guidelines to keep you on track for the day.

What you do to start your day needs to be exactly the same every day. For example, if when your baby wakes for the day, you first change the diaper, then bring the baby to the family bed, and then do your morning feed, then this is exactly what you need to do every morning so that your baby begins to understand that these specific events mean it is the start to the day. This encourages an association to this ritual and starting the day, but the most important part is not the ritual but the leaving of the sleep environment and stimulating the senses with talk, light, and conversation. This lets your baby know it is time to start the day.

Here are some morning routine examples:

- Baby is a nursery sleeper. Walk into the room, turn the lights on, talk, smile, change diaper, cuddle in family bed, and feed.
- Baby is a bed sharer. Feed, change diaper, talk, play, and create a stimulating environment (don't fall back to sleep), and then leave the bed.

CREATING A NIGHTTIME SCHEDULE

Besides introducing a daytime routine, you also need to introduce a bedtime routine. This is similar in concept, except that it *cannot* be changed or altered at all. It needs to be followed 100 percent, no matter what. This routine will be what you do every night before you lay your baby down to sleep and should last somewhere between thirty to forty-five minutes in total. Note that the entire routine should not be any longer than forty-five minutes because that can make it harder to lay the baby down. Babies' sleep cycles are between forty-five and sixty minutes, so they will be coming up on a light stage of sleep just as they are being laid down. I prefer to nurse/feed babies to sleep and transfer them in a nice deep sleep to the sleeping surface.

Whatever you are going to do—read a book, change a diaper, sing a song, change into pajamas, do a full feed (which is absolutely a must), and so forth—you need to do it in the same order every night, and it needs to take less time, combined, than forty-five minutes.

Here are some bedtime routine examples:

- Baby is a nursery sleeper. Go to the nursery, change diaper (I like one size bigger at night to help with absorption), sing a song, read a book, lights out, and feed to sleep.
- Baby is a bed sharer. Go to your room, change the diaper, sing a song, read a book, and lie down together to nurse with lights out. Don't leave unless the edges of the bed will protect your baby from falling. This typically means you need to also go to bed because your baby will roll around looking for milk and needs Mom nearby.

WHAT TIME SHOULD YOU PUT YOUR BABY TO BED?

Take into consideration that babies are developing their circadian rhythms, and bedtime will need to be paired with sunset. The hours you are starting with are one four-hour stretch and working up to a full ten-hour night. Taking all of this into consideration, I tend to prefer an eight to nine o'clock bedtime. This will give you a six to seven o'clock wake time once you have completed Baby Created Sleep training and provide two to three and a half hours per day for naps.

FEEDING SCHEDULE FOR AN EIGHT-POUND BABY

With putting a schedule in place, you always start with bedtime. The schedule below depicts an eight o'clock bedtime and reserves ten hours for nighttime sleep. The reason we have ten hours for night and not twelve is because the normal sleep for a baby past eight weeks is eleven to fourteen hours. Now, there are going to be babies who sleep beyond that range, but for the average baby, we reserve ten hours for night sleep and three to four hours for daytime naps totaling fourteen hours in a twenty-four period. With bedtime being our starting point for the schedule, you will create a routine that is easily repeated, always at the same time, and won't exceed forty-five minutes (this is usually better to do without a bath since they tend to take long and are often more stimulating than soothing).

Equally as important as a bedtime routine is a morning routine. This lets your baby know we are no longer in nighttime sleep, but we are starting our day. In order to effectively do this, you must leave the sleep space at six in the morning. Even if you have to wake your baby, make sure to start the day at six o'clock. Remember, we are building structure with this and will be able to adjust later but have to start somewhere.

You will have the most successful results if you implement your daytime schedule for two full days before implementing any adjustments to your baby's nights.

6:00 a.m. feed (2–4 oz.): Start your day. Morning time will be when you leave the sleep space/nursery. You can cuddle in the family bed or just start your day with a diaper, clothes change, conversation, and stimulation. Just leaving the nursery is enough of an environmental change to know it's not nighttime anymore.

8:00 a.m. feed (2–4 oz.): Nap (Usually one and a half to two hours after they wake up and should start with a feed to ensure a good nap. It can be in any location.)

10:00 a.m. feed (2–4 oz.)

12:00 p.m. feed (2–4 oz.): This will ideally be followed by a nap in the crib.

2:00 p.m. feed (2–4 oz.): Nap

4:00 p.m. feed (2–4 oz.)

6:00 p.m. feed (2–4 oz.): Small catnap to help support evening fussiness. Don't do this nap in the sleep space in order to avoid going into the full nighttime sleep.

8:00 p.m. feed (2–4 oz.): Bedtime. This will be a routine of thirty to forty-five minutes of an easily repeatable routine. For example, this includes a feed, diaper change, pajamas, and song/book in the nursery with a calm, relaxing beginning to the night that will help the transition to night sleep.

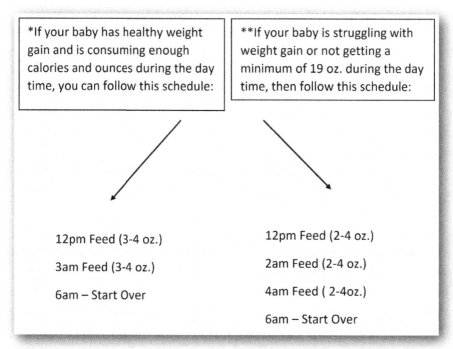

*If your baby has healthy weight gain and is consuming enough calories and ounces during the day time, you can follow this schedule:

12pm Feed (3-4 oz.)

3am Feed (3-4 oz.)

6am – Start Over

**If your baby is struggling with weight gain or not getting a minimum of 19 oz. during the day time, then follow this schedule:

12pm Feed (2-4 oz.)

2am Feed (2-4 oz.)

4am Feed (2-4oz.)

6am – Start Over

*If your baby is capable of transferring 90 ml and is sleeping naturally past two hours, you can feed at 12:00 a.m., 3:00 a.m., and 6:00 a.m. If your baby wakes up before the three-hour mark, then immediately feed.

**If your baby is on the lower side of weight gain or severe reflux, and they have a harder time of transferring the calories from nighttime to the daytime (3–4 oz.), it will be best to feed at 12:00 a.m., 2:00 a.m., 4:00 a.m., and 6:00 a.m. to ensure he or she is getting enough calories.

- Floor activity is ideal, multiple times a day, varying from ten minutes to one hour.
- Naps will be twenty to sixty minutes at a time and will happen four to six times a day.
- Total ounces will need to be 24–28 oz. with formula at 20 cal./oz. (the normal formula on the shelf).
- The feeds will range 2–4 oz. at each feed. Do not expect your baby to eat the exact same amount at each feed.
- There is a possibility your baby will eat every two hours instead of three hours once his or her metabolism has been triggered. For example: 2:00 a.m. feed (2–4 oz.) and 4:00 a.m. feed (2–4 oz.).

TRANSITION ONE: FOUR-HOUR STRETCH AND REMOVAL OF FIRST FEEDING

(minimum age of eight to twelve weeks and minimum of eight pounds)

After you have established solid daytime and bedtime routines, and your baby has become accustomed to these routines, then you can start the transition to one four-hour long stretch (a time without milk) in a twenty-four-hour period. Reserve this stretch for the night (eight o'clock to midnight).

Your baby should already be leaning toward this by occasionally sleeping without waking for milk for longer than two-hour increments. This is because this sleep method is entirely baby created, meaning that you follow your baby's cues. If your baby naturally goes longer than two hours without waking for a feed (before you begin this transition), then this tells you that baby is ready for the first removal of nighttime milk. Keep in mind that your baby must meet the requirements of eight weeks of age and a weight of eight pounds before working on this transition.

This transition should happen without you having to push it. If your baby isn't ready, then your baby isn't ready. Don't force it. You can tell if your baby isn't ready if your baby isn't leaning toward this transition at all, or if you push a feed, and it is extremely difficult for the first three nights and your baby isn't making up the difference in calories in the daytime. You will know within the first two nights whether or not your baby is ready; however, that is fairly rare. If you are listening and paying close attention to your baby's cues, then you should be able to see readiness to move to the next transition. Babies tend to lead you to what is right for them if you let them.

Once your baby is ready to start Transition One, you will put your baby to bed as you normally would (via the bedtime routine). If your baby wakes up two hours after bedtime, do not offer a feeding. Instead, soothe, hold, rock your baby, or do whatever you have to do to get your baby back to sleep without a feed.

It is vital that your baby goes back to sleep! When parents try to soothe their babies and then get tired and eventually cave in and offer milk, they are actually training them to think that they need to work for their food. You absolutely do not want your baby to associate crying with food! To soothe back to sleep, start with the most involved and active form of soothing you have (i.e., holding your baby to your chest while walking around), then slowly pull back with less active soothing techniques, and eventually you might just need to stand next to the crib. (Adopt this method every time you soothe in the night while sleep training.) Then, when your baby wakes up again around midnight, go ahead and feed immediately.

After this, proceed through the rest of the night, as you did before you started the sleep training: offering milk each time your baby wakes to feed in the night, every two or three hours. You will have to do this because by feeding your baby the first time, you woke up the metabolism and started it, which triggers the need for another feeding about two hours later. Also note that the next waking could happen as quickly as thirty minutes later, or it may be two hours. Either way, feed your baby at the second waking.

Then in the morning, turn on lights, change diaper (if this is part of your wake-up routine), and take your baby out of the sleep environment right away. You do not want your baby to start confusing the sleep environment with the daytime environment.

This will all take your baby anywhere from three to five nights to retain. After that, you will need to remain on this transition stage for roughly two weeks. This is important for two reasons. First, it gives your baby time to not only retain this new stretch without milk but also fully adjust to it. Second, it allows your baby the time he or she needs to gain the necessary weight to move to Transition Two.

Here is a step-by-step guide to help transition into one four-hour stretch of sleep without a feed at night. Use this as a general guide to get through each night and what is to be expected.

- Night one
  - Calculate the daytime for calories and total number of hours of naps.
  - Bring milk in case you need it, but the plan is to not use it until the designated feeding time. Try an assortment of soothing techniques to get the baby to go back to sleep without the feed.
  - If breastfeeding, you will not need to bring milk but need to make your breast inaccessible (by covering up with a shirt).
  - Once it reaches midnight, you will resume feedings as scheduled (12:00 a.m., 2:00 a.m., 4:00 a.m.).
  - Once it is morning (six o'clock), *leave* your nursery, and start your daytime schedule.

- Nights two and three
  - Calculate the daytime for calories and total number of hours of naps.
  - Bring milk in case you need it, but the plan is to not use it until the designated feeding time. Try an assortment of soothing techniques to get the baby to go back to sleep without the feed.

- Nights two and three are typically the most difficult nights and require extensive soothing. The most important thing to remember with pushing a feed and soothing is that you get your baby back to sleep without food. If you soothe for twenty-five minutes and get tired, and this results in feeding, you will create a very negative association to food and crying for your baby.
- If breastfeeding, you will not need to bring milk but need to make your breast inaccessible.
- Once it reaches midnight, you will resume feedings as scheduled (12:00 a.m., 2:00 a.m., 4:00 a.m.).
- Once it's morning (six o'clock) *leave* your nursery, and start your day schedule.

- Nights four and five
  - Calculate the daytime for calories and total number of hours of naps.
  - Soothe as needed.
  - Once it reaches midnight, you will resume feedings as scheduled (12:00 a.m., 2:00 a.m., 4:00 a.m.).
  - Once it is morning (six o'clock), *leave* your nursery, and start your day schedule.

Before moving into the next transition (i.e., a longer stretch without milk at night), your baby will need to have gained two pounds and weigh a minimum of ten pounds. A baby gains, on average, about half a pound a week, so, if your baby follows this trend, you will stay on the first stretch (and each thereafter) for about four weeks. Do not start the second stretch until your baby weighs at least ten pounds!

CASE STUDY ONE

Mom gave birth to a 5 lb., 13 oz. sweet baby girl at full term—forty weeks. They've learned a lot in the first few weeks about how to best care for their baby, Kimmy. Mom and Dad just met with the pediatrician for their eight-week checkup. At their appointment, they were told that Kimmy has healthy growth, a clean bill of health, and is currently 8 lb., 12 oz. The pediatrician is comfortable with them pushing for one four-hour stretch of sleep in a twenty-four-hour period.

When Mom and Dad get home, they decide to start by filling out a forty-eight-hour log. That way they are able to make sure that Kimmy is consuming 24–25 oz. a day, which is around five hundred calories. Mom is combination feeding their little girl: some feeds are breast milk and some are with formula. Currently, they find that Kimmy is eating every two hours during the day and every two and a half hours at nighttime. The nighttime feeds are given by Dad from a bottle and range from 60 ml to 120 ml. She currently sleeps in a Rock 'n Play sleeper in the parents' room. Mom and Dad would like to keep her in their bedroom while starting sleep training.

Night one is to put a Pack 'n Play or crib in the parents' room and transition baby girl to sleeping on a flat surface. Ideally this is close to the parents' bed. They also are building a healthy bedtime routine that starts promptly at eight o'clock. They go into the bedroom, change her diaper, put her in her pajamas, sing a song, and read two books. Mom then nurses Kimmy to sleep and lays Kimmy down, making sure to not trigger Kimmy's Moro reflex. Kimmy wakes at ten thirty; Mom soothes her back to sleep. Her second wake is at 11:55 p.m.; Mom then feeds her.

Nights two and three, Dad does the soothing when Kimmy wakes at eleven and notices that she does better when he holds his hand on her chest and gently rocks back and forth. They also notice that Kimmy sleeps more soundly when sleeping in bed with Mom and Dad, starting at two in the morning until they start their day at six o'clock. With all of the other feeds, it allows Mom and baby to sleep more peacefully when lying next to each other.

After five nights, Kimmy has adjusted fully to her new schedule! Mom and Dad have successfully completed Transition One. This is a great starting point since baby girl is still so little. Even if she tries to sleep longer than four hours, they won't let her because it is important to have her continue to gain weight in order to move on with sleep training. Now that baby girl is doing one long stretch, each of her daytime feeds needs to be a minimum of 60–90 ml in order to maintain healthy weight gain and development. Mom and Dad will continue with this routine until their baby is at least 10 lb. and is ready for Transition Two.

TRANSITION TWO

TWELVE WEEKS, TEN POUNDS: SIX-HOUR STRETCH

THE AMOUNT OF changes you have experienced with your baby has been nearly on a daily basis at this point, but now you will start to see things fall into place and show a bit of a routine. Not the type of routine you can depend on daily, but definitely moving toward separating day from night instead of a twenty-four-hour schedule. This is due to the final and third stage of the circadian rhythms being developed (which is your baby's ability to distinctively separate day from night, using sunrise and sunset). With these newly developed skills, your baby is very sensitive and slightly unreliable and will need to be supported.

This is truly a beginning step; just choose a bedtime and a routine to follow. The bedtime should be chosen based on eventually getting to a nine- to ten-hour night. One day your little one will reach a twelve-hour night, but it is not going to happen until he or she is a toddler and sleep has shifted from the day into the night. Your baby's body needs to get a healthy balance between caloric intake, total sleep, and total floor time, so for now we put things into place to support today and what your baby can do exactly where he or she is at. This is followed up with things to put into place to support the next step. For now, thinking of nights in ten-hour blocks, I prefer eight in the evening to six in the morning.

Make sure your baby is ready for Transition Two of sleep support by using the following checklist:

☐ My baby is at least ten pounds.

☐ My baby is *not* sick.

☐ My baby has not had a vaccination within the last forty-eight hours.

☐ My baby has successfully completed Transition One.

Now that you've made sure your little one is ready for Transition Two you can begin sleep training. Here is a general daytime schedule for a ten-pound baby that will allow for enough nap time and calories to support healthy sleeping at night.

DAYTIME SCHEDULE FOR A TEN-POUND BABY

You can modify this schedule to include naps, play and floor time, and so forth. It is meant to be an outline. Please understand that feeds vary from one to three hours apart, and you do not want to exceed a three-hour period.

6:00 a.m. feed (2–4 oz.): Start your day. Morning time will be when you leave the sleep space/nursery. You can cuddle in the family bed or just start your day with a diaper and clothes change, conversation, and stimulation. Just leaving the nursery is enough of an environmental change to know it's not nighttime anymore.

8:00 a.m. feed (2–4 oz.): This will ideally be followed by a nap and is usually one and a half to two hours after baby's first wake. It's best to start with a feed to ensure a good nap.

10:00 a.m. feed (2–4 oz.)

12:00 p.m. feed (2–4 oz.): This will ideally be followed by a nap in the crib.

2:00 p.m. feed (2–4 oz.)

4:00 p.m. feed (2–4 oz.)

6:00 p.m. feed (2–4 oz.): Small catnap to help support evening fussiness. Don't do this nap in the sleep space in order to avoid going into a full night's sleep.

8:00 p.m. feed (2–4 oz.): Bedtime. This will be a routine of thirty to forty-five minutes of an easily repeatable routine. The feeds, diaper change, pajamas, and song/book will be in the nursery with a calm, relaxing beginning to the night, helping the transition to night sleep.

2:00 a.m. feed (2–4 oz.)

4:00 a.m. feed (2–4 oz.)

KEY POINTS

- Floor activity will be ideally multiple times daily, ranging from ten minutes to one hour. It is okay if your baby doesn't love tummy time; still, try it a few times a day. Floor time is considered playing on a flat surface, mastering his or her body movement and control; it's not only tummy time.
- Naps will range from twenty to sixty minutes at a time and will happen four to six times daily.
- Total feeding will need to be 24–28 oz. with formula at 20 cal/oz. (the normal formula on the shelf). The most accurate way to get your baby's daily caloric needs will be to use the following formula:
  - Weight × 55 = calories needed
- The feeds will range 2–4 oz. It is okay if your baby does not eat the exact same amount at each feed.
- Make sure to *keep* the 4:00 a.m. and 6:00 a.m. feed. It is important not to skip these because six o'clock must remain the beginning of your next day, and the baby cannot go from two to six o'clock without a feed.
- Count your daily totals to make sure your baby is staying on track. The exact time of each is less relevant than the grand total for the twenty-four-hour period.
  - Total naps: two and a half to four hours
  - Total floor time: four to six hours

- Total food: weight × 55 = calories needed
  - To get ounces from this, you will take calories needed and divide by 22 for breast milk and 20–24 for formula, depending on which type is being used.
  - An example would be
    - 10 lb. × 55 = 550 cal
    - 550 cal / 22 cal/oz. = 25 oz.
    - An amount of 25 oz. is what your baby needs per twenty-four hours.
    - Keep in mind some babies will take more ounces.

TRANSITION TWO: SIX-HOUR STRETCH AND REMOVAL OF THE SECOND FEEDING

The second transition follows the same ideology as the first. This stretch will occur when your baby weighs at least ten pounds and is naturally leaning toward a longer stretch at night. The baby shows signs of this by occasionally sleeping for longer than four-hour stretches in the night without waking for a feed. It will feel like a spontaneous occurrence and usually only happens one night out of the week, but this is your signal. Again, this method is baby created, so be prepared to follow your baby's readiness for the next transition.

To help your baby into this stretch, use the same push technique you used for the first transition. Remember, it will be easier to stay in the nursery for the first three nights of each transition because you will want to be quick to respond to your baby's wakes. It is normal that baby will wake often for the first few nights as you are changing what his or her nighttime used to look like. This will also affect what his or her days look like. Your baby may need additional feeds, naps, and cuddles during the day.

Your little one will be looking to you for guidance as you teach him or her what sleep is. This is done by remaining calm while soothing. You should keep your eyes closed, act sleepy, and do not talk to your baby. The more support you give, the easier each transition will be. Remember, you are not limiting your soothing. The only thing you are doing is taking away feeds at night.

If you are starting now, go through the checklist presented a few pages back to ensure readiness, and begin as follows. When your baby wakes in the first six hours from bedtime (give or take), don't feed. Instead, soothe your baby back to sleep. In order for this to work, your baby has to go back to sleep. At baby's next wake, go ahead and feed him or her. This waking will likely occur around two in the morning. You will then feed again at four o'clock, even if baby is sleeping. It is important not to skip this feed; baby will need these calories to sustain the longer stretch from eight in the evening until two in the morning without a feed.

This transition, just as the last one, should take three to five nights for your baby to retain and give you approximately a six-hour stretch without waking for milk at night.

With this transition, it is even more important that you focus on your baby's daytime caloric intake. You are now at the point where the calories that were once being received during the night absolutely need to be replaced during the day. If these calories are lost, it will make a big difference in your baby's growth and development. So, remember to feed at 2:00 a.m., 4:00 a.m., and at the start of your day at 6:00 a.m.

The tools you are working on with your baby are to help create happy and healthy associations that will support your baby's development of sleep and growth.

You are creating the following associations:

- Establishing a bedtime, which lets your baby and his or her body know when to go into a deeper, more restful, and repairing sleep.
- Establishing morning time, which is the association your baby will have to the end of night and beginning of a day full of activity, learning, and fun.
- Establishing soothing, with the pulling of milk but full support with other soothing techniques. You are showing your baby that

he or she is being supported by his or her parents. Milk is a source of nutrients to the body—a requirement of survival. It is also very comforting and soothing to any human. But there are other options for the same love, support, and comfort that are important to find for your child.

- Establishing a six-hour stretch allows your baby's body to repair and rest, giving his or her metabolism and digestive system a break.

Here is a step-by-step guide for working through Transition Two. Remember to begin with your daytime schedule, and give it two full days before pushing for longer stretches at night. It's also a good idea to assess your nursery/sleep space to ensure you are promoting healthy sleep.

- Night one
    - Calculate daily totals for calories, floor time, and hours for daytime naps.
    - Bring milk (water/formula) to be made in the nursery in case you need it, but the plan is to not use it until the designated feeding time.
    - If breastfeeding, you will not need to bring milk but need to make your breast inaccessible.
    - Try an assortment of soothing techniques to get the baby to go back to sleep without milk until two o'clock.
    - Once it is past two o'clock, you will resume feedings as scheduled (2:00 a.m., 4:00 a.m.).
    - Once it is morning (six o'clock), *leave* your sleep space (nursery, parents' room, etc.), and start your day schedule.
    - It is important you soothe your baby back to sleep, and then when he or she wakes, go for the feed. If you are in the middle of a wake and it is two o'clock, do not go for the

feed despite it being the six-hour mark. We do not want to create a negative association that your baby has to cry for milk.

- Nights two and three
  - Calculate daily totals for calories, floor time, and hours for daytime naps.
  - Bring milk (water/formula) to be made in the nursery in case you need it, but the plan is to not use it until the designated feeding time.
  - If breastfeeding, you will not need to bring milk but need to make your breast inaccessible.
  - Try an assortment of soothing techniques to get the baby to go back to sleep without milk until two o'clock.
  - Nights two and three are typically the most difficult nights and require extensive soothing.

    The most important thing to remember with pushing a feed and soothing is that you get your baby back to sleep without food. If you soothe for twenty-five minutes and get tired and this results in feeding your baby, you will create a very negative association to food and crying for your baby.
  - Once it is past two o'clock, you will resume feedings as scheduled (2:00 a.m., 4:00 a.m.)
  - Once it is morning (six o'clock), *leave* your sleep space (nursery, parents' room, etc.), and start your day schedule.
  - It is so very important that you soothe your baby back to sleep and then, when he or she wakes, go for the feed. If you are in the middle of a wake and it is two o'clock, do not go for the feed despite it being the six-hour mark. We do not want to create a negative association that your baby has to cry for milk.

- Nights four and five
  - Calculate daily totals for calories, floor time, and hours for daytime naps.
  - Soothe as needed.
  - Once it is past two o'clock, you will resume feedings as scheduled (2:00 a.m., 4:00 a.m.).
  - Once it is morning (six o'clock), *leave* your nursery, and start your day schedule.

The next transition will happen based on weight gain, but to maintain this progress, you must stick with your daytime schedule and forms of soothing at night as needed. Now that you have conquered six-hour nights, allow your baby to maintain this stretch until he or she is ready to move forward to the eight-hour nights. Relax and enjoy your little one and how quickly he or she is coming along.

The best ways to support the preparation for your eight-hour nights are as follows:

1) Maintain the six-hour nights. This sounds simple enough, but there is a two- to three-week transition period. Your first five nights of accomplishing this transition are the nights you have a set plan and are focused on calories. The first week following, you will have a few nights (one to three) out of your seven-night week that you have night wake before the six-hour stretch, so make sure you soothe and keep all of your schedule in place. The third week will show even better results, and the night that you have an early wake, make sure you keep the six-hour stretch in place without milk.
2) If your baby has had a low caloric intake for the day, it is vital he or she makes up the calories at night; they can't be lost for proper growth.
   a. This would look like the following:

✓ Total floor time: five hours

✓ Total naps: three hours, fifteen minutes

✓ Total ounces: 16 oz. (We want at least 18 oz. with 6 oz. split between the two and four o'clock feeds.)

b. We can see that our day was great, excluding the total amount of milk. This doesn't mean we need a feed before the six-hour mark, but it does mean we need at least 8 oz. of milk between two and five o'clock before the day starts at six o'clock (this is a feed we use for the next day's calculation). The easiest way to split this would be 4 oz. at two o'clock and 4 oz. at four o'clock.

3) Floor time will need to increase at three months. To get to four hours a day at twelve weeks is great, but to help yourself prepare for your next stretch, continue to work on increasing this to six hours a day.

4) Keep in mind a growth spurt is common around four months, and this will require more calories and more sleep for a period of five to seven days.

5) Naps are not yet consolidated, so keep up with the small catnaps, and don't worry that your baby may only sleep twenty to thirty minutes at a time. It is normal! The accumulated total hours of daytime naps are what matters when considering sleep training.

6) Your baby is the only one who can tell you when he or she is ready to move forward, so read his or her cues, and follow your instincts.

7) At first, six hours of sleep will sound like heaven, but quickly you will realize that a feed at two, four, and six o'clock is not the easiest thing to keep up with. Remember we do this to ensure calories and to create structure for the night that your baby's body can handle. So stay patient, and know the eight-hour stretch will offer more relief, but for now go to bed when your baby does to ensure you get your six hours of sleep.

TROUBLESHOOTING

1. Is your baby very restless and fidgety during sleep?
   a. This can be a sign of too little floor time during the day, in which case you can up your floor time the following day and see quick results.
2. Is your baby showing signs of hunger shortly after a feed?
   a. This can be a sign of low calories per ounce in the milk.
      i. For breast milk, you will need to increase the fat intake in your diet and look for a thick layer of fat separation on the top after being in the refrigerator for twenty-four hours. Ideally this layer should be so thick that when you tilt the bottle from side to side, there is resistance, and the layer is solid across the entire top.
      ii. For formula, you will need to look at the calories per ounce in the nutrition facts on the back of the container. You will want it to be at least 20 cal./oz.
3. Is your baby waking up at two o'clock and is wide awake laughing, smiling, and seemingly ready to start the day?
   a. This is often a sign of too many daytime hours of sleep being taken up and not reserving enough for nighttime.
4. Lights on or lights off?
   a. It is imperative that *all* lights be off in the room. This includes lights to sound machines, humidifiers, hallways, monitors, and so forth. At this stage, babies' circadian rhythms are highly sensitive and fairly underdeveloped. Any light will disrupt this and directly affect their nighttime sleep. Cognitively, they are not able to understand fear, so they are not yet afraid of the dark. Therefore, it is important you are familiar with the layout of the nursery, so you are able to navigate without any sort of lighting.

CASE STUDY TWO

Jack was born at thirty-seven weeks and was 6 lb., 2 oz. at birth. He has had a hard time with weight gain and was transferred to an amino-acid-based formula due to a severe whey protein allergy and reflux. His weight gain has been slow, and he has had a hard time getting to this point of finally being able to eat without pain. Jack is now twelve weeks old and weighs 10 lb., 5 oz. In the past three weeks, his weight gain has been amazing, and both parents and Jack's pediatrician believe he will be able to continue healthy growth and development and can begin sleep training.

Jack's parents have also noticed a change in his sleep. He has on occasion slept up to five hours a night, which is a first for them. After looking into the Baby Created Sleep method, they feel he is ready to try for a six-hour nighttime stretch.

They begin with reviewing his log that they have been keeping to make sure he is reaching his goals for floor time, naps, and calories. Jack has never had a set bedtime before now and has never slept on a flat surface (due to his severe reflux). His parents start with daytime naps in his crib, sleeping flat, and a set bedtime with a routine at eight o'clock for three days. They also focus on increasing his floor time and calories for the day to prepare for Transition Two.

It is day four, and things have been going very well, so they plan on beginning Transition Two tonight. The first night Jack does great! They only had to soothe him one time before the six-hour mark and resumed feeds at 2:00 a.m., 4:00 a.m., and 6:00 a.m. The following day they noticed he was a little extrasleepy and hungry but overall very happy. On night two, Jack woke up multiple times before two o'clock and required more soothing. The following day, he was extrasleepy and very hungry.

On night three, things were wonderful, but they noticed after the two o'clock feed that Jack's reflux bothered him. To help support this, they had Jack sleep in an elevated position from two until six in the morning. What worked best for Jack was continuing the nights with a flat-surface sleeping from eight in the evening until two in the morning, and then in an elevated sleeping position after food had been introduced into the metabolism.

TRANSITION THREE

TWELVE POUNDS AND OVER TWELVE WEEKS: DOWN TO ONE FEED A NIGHT

YOUR BABY MAY reach this weight marker before twelve weeks, in which case you'd wait until twelve weeks to allow the development of the circadian rhythms to finalize the third stage of development (which is your baby's ability to distinctively separate day from night using sunrise and sunset). With these newly developed skills, your baby is very sensitive and will need to be supported by you as the parent. At twelve pounds, your baby is able to go one six- to eight-hour stretch of sleep in a twenty-four-hour period.

Developmentally, your baby is now showing much more controlled movements and upper-body strength. He or she is giggly, making eye contact, and showing you his or her cute personality. If you are exactly at twelve weeks, you may be encountering a growth spurt, which isn't the ideal timing for starting a transition. It lasts five to seven days, and your baby will be eating and sleeping more. Your baby may increase his or her calories significantly at this time but won't likely keep them this high, but will instead resume to a similar amount that he or she was at, prior to the growth spurt (24–30 oz.).

DEVELOPMENTAL PROGRESSION

At four months, your baby should do the following:

- Smile spontaneously.
- Enjoy playing with other people and may be upset when the playing stops.

- Begin to imitate some of the facial expressions of the adults around him or her.
- Start to babble.
- Start to mimic different sounds heard around him or her.
- Have different types of cries that are distinguishable.
- Show emotions such as happy or sad.
- Respond to affection.
- Reach for toys with a single hand.
- Develop hand-eye coordination.
- Follow things that move from side to side with his or her eyes.
- Pay close attention to people's faces.
- Have increased recognition of family members and objects at a distance.
- Hold his or her head steady without any support.
- Push down his or her legs when the feet are on a hard surface.
- Be able to—or at least be attempting to—roll over from the stomach to the back.
- Hold and shake toys without a problem.

Here are some red flags to be aware of at the four-month mark:

- Baby isn't watching things with his or her eyes as the objects move.
- Baby doesn't smile at people.
- Baby can't hold his or her head steady.
- Baby doesn't "coo" or make different sounds.
- Baby isn't bringing his or her hands or other objects to his or her mouth.
- Baby isn't pushing down with the legs when the feet are on a hard surface.
- Baby has difficulty moving one or both of his or her eyes in any direction.

Make sure your baby is ready for Transition Three of sleep training by following this checklist.

- ☐ My baby is at least twelve pounds.
- ☐ My baby is *not* sick.
- ☐ My baby has not had a vaccination within the last forty-eight hours.
- ☐ My baby has successfully completed Transition Two.

If you have checked all of these items, then you are ready to start Transition Three. If this is your first transition, remember to begin with your daytime schedule and give it two full days before beginning nights. It is also a good idea to assess your nursery/sleep space to ensure you are promoting healthy and safe sleep. Here is a general guideline for a daytime schedule for a twelve-pound baby. This schedule will help to ensure enough nap time, floor time, and feeds to promote longer sleep at night.

DAYTIME SCHEDULE FOR A TWELVE-POUND BABY

You can modify this schedule to include naps, play and floor time, and so forth. This is meant to be an outline. Also note that feeds will vary between two and three hours throughout the day and that the main goal is total caloric intake, and for breastfeeding we will be focusing on weekly weight gain.

6:00 a.m. feed (2–4 oz.): Start your day. Morning time will be when you leave the sleep space/nursery. You can cuddle in the family bed or just start your day with a diaper change, clothes change, conversation, and stimulation. Just leaving the nursery is enough of an environmental change to know it's not nighttime anymore.

8:00 a.m. feed (2–4 oz.): Nap. (Should be between one and a half to two hours after you start your day and is best if you start with a feed.)

10:00 a.m. feed (2–4 oz.)

12:00 p.m. feed (2–4 oz.): This will ideally be followed by a nap in the crib.

2:00 p.m. feed (2–4 oz.)

4:00 p.m. feed (2–4 oz.)

6:00 p.m. feed (2–4 oz.): Small catnap to help support evening fussiness. Don't do this nap in the sleep space in order to avoid going into a full night's sleep.

8:00 p.m. feed (2–4 oz.): Bedtime. This will be a routine of thirty to forty-five minutes of an easily repeatable routine. The feeds, diaper change, pajamas, and song/book will be in the nursery or sleep space with a calm, relaxing beginning to the night, helping the transition to night sleep.

Between 3:30 and 4:00 a.m. feed (2–4 oz.)

KEY POINTS

- Floor activity will be ideally multiple times a day of ten minutes to one hour a day. It is okay if your baby doesn't love tummy time, but try it a few times a day, and know that most of this time will be spent with the baby on his or her back. Floor time is playing on a flat surface, mastering and controlling his or her body movement; it's not only tummy time.
- Naps will be twenty to sixty minutes at a time and will happen four to six times a day.
- Total feeding will need to be at least 26–30 oz. with formula at 20 cal/oz. (the normal formula on the shelf). The most accurate way to get your baby's daily caloric needs will be
  - weight × 55 = calories needed
- The feeds will range 2–4 oz. Do not expect your baby to eat the exact same amount at each feed.
- Make sure to *keep* the four and six o'clock feeds. It is important not to skip these because six o'clock must remain the beginning

of your next day, and the baby cannot go past four o'clock because the feed will be too close to the morning feed.

- Count your daily totals to make sure your baby is staying on track. The exact time of each is less relevant than the grand total for the twenty-four-hour period.
  - Total naps: two and a half to four hours.
  - Total floor time: four to six hours.
  - Total food: weight × 55 = calories needed.
    - To get ounces from this, you will take calories needed and divide by 22 for breast milk and 20–24 for formula, depending on the formula being used.
    - An example would be
      - 12 lb. × 55 = 660 cal
      - 660 cal / 22 cal/oz. = 30 oz.
      - An amount of 30 oz. is what your baby needs per twenty-four hours.
      - Keep in mind some babies will take more.

TRANSITION THREE: EIGHT-HOUR STRETCH AND DOWN TO ONE NIGHTTIME FEED

This stretch follows the same plan of the Baby Created Sleep method. This stretch will occur when your baby weighs at least twelve pounds and is naturally leaning toward a longer stretch at night. You baby shows signs of this by occasionally sleeping for longer periods in the night without waking for milk. It will feel like a spontaneous occurrence and usually only happens one night out of the week, but this is your signal. Again, this method is baby created, so just be prepared to follow your baby's readiness for a longer stretch at night.

To help your baby into this stretch, use the same push technique you used for the first two transitions. If you are starting with this transition, go through the checklist presented a few pages back to ensure readiness and begin as follows.

When your baby wakes within the first eight hours from bedtime (give or take), don't feed. Instead, soothe your baby back to sleep. In order for this to work, your baby *has* to go back to sleep with the soothing and not with milk. You will spend the duration of the night with your baby to ensure you are quick to respond to a wake and provide a very high level of support. Your baby will wake at times before the four o'clock feed and look to you for guidance. With your body language and entire aura, you will be able to communicate to your baby that you are there for soothing and support and that he or she is not alone. The days following this new transition will require extra feeds and extra naps as your baby's body is adjusting.

As with the previous transition, it is extremely important to focus on your baby's daytime caloric intake. Without enough calories during the day, it will be difficult to push for an eight-hour stretch without a feed at night and will impact your little one's growth and development with the loss of calories.

The tools you are working on with your baby are to create happy and healthy associations that will support his or her development of sleep and growth.

You are creating these associations:

- Establishing a bedtime, which lets baby and his or her body know when to go into a deeper, more restful, and repairing sleep.
- Establishing morning time, which is the association your baby will have to the end of night and beginning of a day full of activity, learning, and fun.
- Establishing soothing, with the pulling of milk but full support with other soothing techniques. You are showing your baby that he or she is being supported by his or her parents. Milk is a source of nutrients to the body—a requirement of survival. It is also very comforting and soothing to any human. But there are other options for the same love, support, and comfort that are important to find for your child.

- Establishing an eight-hour stretch, which gives your baby's metabolism and digestive system a break and allows sleep-wake homeostasis to start the body to repair and rest with full sleep cycles. This is the time for your baby to get one long stretch of sleep.

Here is a step-by-step guide for Transition Three. Use this as an outline for what each of your nights will look like. It will give you an idea of what to expect with each night and pointers to keep you on track through sleep training.

- Night one
  - Calculate the daytime for total calories, total floor time, and total number of hours of naps.
  - Bring milk (water/formula) to be made in the nursery in case you need it, but the plan is to not use it until the designated feeding time.
  - If breastfeeding, you will not need to bring milk but need to make your breast inaccessible.
  - Try an assortment of soothing techniques to get the baby to go back to sleep without milk until four o'clock.
  - Once it is four o'clock, you feed and then resume feedings as scheduled (6:00 a.m.).
  - Once it is morning (six o'clock), *leave* your sleep space (nursery, parents' room, etc.), and start your day schedule.
  - It is important you soothe your baby back to sleep, and then when he or she wakes, go for the feed. If you are in the middle of a wake and it is four o'clock, do not go for the feed despite it being the eight-hour mark. We do not want to create a negative association that your baby has to cry for milk.
  - Once it is four o'clock, you will offer a full feed. This must be offered with a bottle so that you can measure the amount

your little one is consuming at this feed and ensure it is a full feed. You can't go past four o'clock because it will affect your daytime schedule. This may result in you waking your baby to feed.

- Nights two and three
  - Calculate the daytime for total calories, total floor time, and total number of hours of naps.
  - Bring milk (water/formula) to be made in the nursery in case you need it, but the plan is to not use it until the designated feeding time.
  - If breastfeeding, you will not need to bring milk but need to make your breast inaccessible.
  - Try an assortment of soothing techniques to get the baby to go back to sleep without milk until four o'clock.
  - Once it is four o'clock, you will feed and then resume feedings as scheduled (6:00 a.m.).
  - Once it is morning (six o'clock), *leave* your sleep space (nursery, parents' room, etc.) and start your day schedule.
  - It's very important you soothe your baby back to sleep, and then when he or she wakes, go for the feed. If you are in the middle of a wake and it is four o'clock, do not go for the feed despite it being the eight-hour mark. We do not want to create a negative association that your baby has to cry for milk.
  - Nights two and three are typically the most difficult nights and require extensive soothing.

    The most important thing to remember with pushing a feed and soothing is that you get your baby back to sleep without food. If you soothe for twenty-five minutes and get tired and this results in feeding your baby, you will create a very negative association to food and crying for your baby. Instead stay calm, and focus on the support you are giving your baby to get back to sleep.

- Once it is four o'clock, you will offer a full feed. This must be offered with a bottle so that you can measure the amount your little one is consuming at this feed and ensure it is a full feed. You can't go past four o'clock because it will affect your daytime schedule. This may result in you waking your baby to feed.

- Nights four and five
  - Calculate the daytime for total calories, total floor time, and total number of hours of naps.
  - Soothe as needed.
  - Once it is past four o'clock, you will feed and then resume feedings as scheduled (6:00 a.m.).
  - Once it is morning (six o'clock), *leave* your nursery, and start your day schedule.

The next transition will happen based on weight gain, but to maintain this progress, you must stick with your daytime schedule and forms of soothing at night as needed. The first five nights are the toughest. Over the next three weeks, you will have one to two nights of the week when you have an earlier wake and need to soothe before the four o'clock feeding.

TIPS TO HELP PREPARE FOR YOUR NEXT STEP

Now that you have conquered eight-hour nights, allow your baby to maintain this stretch until he or she is ready to move forward to the nine- to ten-hour nights. Relax and enjoy your little one and how quickly he or she is coming along. The best ways to support the preparation for your nine- to ten-hour nights are as follows:

1. Maintain the eight-hour nights. This sounds simple enough, but there is a two- to three-week transition period. Your first five

nights of accomplishing this transition are the nights you have a set plan and are focused on calories. The following first week, you will have a few nights (one to three) out of your seven-night week that you have night wake before the eight-hour mark, so make sure you soothe and keep all of your schedule in place. The third week will show even better results, and the night that you have an early wake, make sure you keep the eight hours in place without milk.

2. If your baby has had a low caloric intake for the day, it is vital that he or she makes up the calories at night; they can't be lost for proper growth.

   a. This would look like the following:
      i   ✓ Total floor time: five hours
      ii. ✓ Total naps: three hours, fifteen minutes
      iii. ✗ Total ounces: 20 oz. (This is under the daily requirement; we want at least 24 oz.).
         i. We can see that our day was great, excluding the total amount of milk. This doesn't mean we need a feed before the eight-hour mark, but it does mean we need at least 4 oz. of milk between three thirty and four o'clock before the day starts at six (this is a feed we use for the next day's calculation). The easiest way to do this would be 4 oz. at four o'clock.

3. Floor time will need to increase between three months and on. To get to four hours a day at twelve weeks is great, but to help yourself prepare for your next stretch, continue to work on increasing this to six hours a day.

4. Keep in mind a growth spurt is common around four months, and this will require more calories and sleep for a period of five to seven days.

5. Naps are not yet consolidated so for now keep strong with the small catnaps, and don't worry that your baby only sleeps twenty to thirty minutes at a time. It is normal.

6. Your baby is the only one who can tell you when he or she is ready to move forward, so read his or her cues, and follow your instincts.

7. At first, eight hours of sleep will sound like heaven, but quickly you will realize that a feed at four and six o'clock is not the easiest thing to keep up with. Remember we do this to ensure calories and to create structure for the night that your baby's body can handle. So stay patient, and know the nine- to ten-hour stretch will offer more relief, and for now go to bed when your baby does to ensure you get your eight hours of sleep.

8. Having your baby sleep on a flat surface is important by this age, especially if it is part of your long-term goals to have night sleep in the crib.

The next transition will happen based on weight gain, but to maintain this progress, you must stick with your daytime schedule and forms of soothing at night as needed.

TROUBLESHOOTING

1. Is your baby very restless and fidgety during sleep?
    a. This can be a sign of too little floor time during the day, in which case you can up your floor time the following day and see quick results.
    b. It may also be that your baby just needs to be repositioned. Can you imagine how frustrating it would be to not be able to move at your own will when your arm falls asleep? Ugh, the thought is daunting in itself. So simply moving your baby to a new position may be all he or she needs.
2. Is your baby showing signs of hunger shortly after a feed?
    a. This can be a sign of low calories per ounce in the milk.
        i. For breast milk, you will need to increase the fat intake in your diet and look for a thick layer of fat separation

on the top after being in the refrigerator for thirty-four hours. Ideally this layer is so thick when tilting the bottle from side to side that there is resistance and the layer is solid across the entire top.

    ii. For formula, you will need to look at the calories per ounce in the nutrition facts on the back of the container. You will want it to be at least 20 cal/oz.

3. Is your baby waking up at two in the morning and is wide awake laughing, smiling, and seemingly ready to start the day?

    a. This is often a sign of too many daytime hours of sleep being taken up and not reserving enough for nighttime.

4. Is your baby starting to roll over?

    a. If your baby is not yet barrel rolling, don't try to unswaddle. This milestone is a great way for your baby to master his or her body movement and choose his or her own sleep position. An alternative option while your baby is still mastering rolling would be to double swaddle. You will only be double swaddling until baby can move freely. You want him or her to be so efficient that he or she can roll in his or her sleep… literally.

CASE STUDY THREE

Mackenzie was thirty-nine weeks and weighed 6 lb., 4 oz. She is exclusively breastfed and has gained weight well. She is now fourteen weeks, and her parents have already done Transitions One and Two to put in place a set bedtime and the first six-hour stretch at night. They also know the soothing techniques that best support Mackenzie during her transitions. Mackenzie has begun doing longer stretches on her own for the past week, and her parents know this is a sign that she is ready to move to Transition Three.

They begin increasing her day feeds by adding in an evening feed between five and eight o'clock, encouraging cluster feeding before bedtime. After two days of this, they start night one of Transition Three. It goes well, but they only made it to three o'clock instead of the planned four in the morning feed.

On night two, they have multiple wakes, and they take turns for which parent is going in for soothing. By night three, they realize Dad is more successful with soothing, and Mom can sleep from bedtime until feeding at four o'clock, and then Dad brings Mackenzie to Mom in the family bed to nurse. With Dad sleeping in the room until four, Mackenzie has an easier time being soothed by Dad since Mom usually breastfeeds her, so this was confusing for Mackenzie.

By night four, things were going very smoothly, and by night five, Dad goes back to sleeping in his own room and getting Mackenzie at four to bring her to Mom for feeding. They started the week with Mackenzie being 12 lb., 9 oz. and did a weight check at day five to see how she did. She is now 12 lb., 13 oz. This is wonderful weight gain, showing both parents that Mackenzie was able to successfully transfer the calories she needs into the daytime while maintaining proper weight gain.

TRANSITION FOUR

FIFTEEN POUNDS: YAY, FOR A FULL NIGHT'S SLEEP!

YOU HAVE MADE it; your little one and you have been on a beautiful journey so far with so many new skills. A full night's sleep sounds too good to be true, but it's not. This transition will fully separate your days from your nights and is meant to take place when your baby is ready. With a very active and curious little one, your days are full of adventures, and your nights can now be full of sleep.

Go through this final checklist to make sure your baby is ready for Transition Four of sleep training.

- ☐ My baby is at least fifteen pounds.
- ☐ My baby is *not* sick.
- ☐ My baby has not had a vaccination within the last forty-eighty hours.
- ☐ My baby has successfully completed Transition Three.

If you have checked all of these items, then you are ready to start the final stage of sleep training your little one! At this point, your baby should be fifteen pounds and can now go one ten-hour stretch in a twenty-four-hour period without a feed. You can use the following schedule as a guideline to ensure you are supporting your little one with enough calories during the day to allow for a longer stretch at night.

DAYTIME SCHEDULE FOR A FIFTEEN-POUND BABY

You can modify this schedule to include naps, play and floor time, and so forth. This is meant to be an outline. Also note that feeds will vary between two and three hours throughout the day, and the main goal is total caloric intake, and for breastfeeding we will be focusing on weekly weight gain.

6:00 a.m. feed (2–4 oz.): Start your day. Morning time will be when you leave the sleep space/nursery. You can cuddle in the family bed or just start your day with a diaper change, clothes change, conversation, and stimulation. Just leaving the nursery is enough of an environmental change to know it's not nighttime anymore.

8:00 a.m. feed (2–4 oz.): Nap. (Should be about one and a half to two hours after you start your day and is best if given with a feed.)

10:00 a.m. feed (2–4 oz.)

12:00 p.m. feed (2–4 oz.): This will ideally be followed by a nap in the crib.

2:00 p.m. feed (2–4 oz.)

4:00 p.m. feed (2–4 oz.)

6:00 p.m. feed (2–4 oz.): Small catnap to help support evening fussiness. Don't do this nap in the sleep space in order to avoid going into a full night's sleep.

8:00 p.m. feed (2–4 oz.): Bedtime. This will be a routine of thirty to forty-five minutes of an easily repeatable routine. The feeds, diaper change, pajamas, and song/book will be in the nursery or sleep space with a calm, relaxing beginning to the night, helping the transition to night sleep.

4:00 a.m. feed (2 oz.) to no feed

KEY POINTS

- Floor activity is ideally multiple times a day of ten minutes to one hour a day. It is okay if your baby doesn't love tummy time;

continue to try it a few times a day. Most of the floor time will be spent on his or her back. Floor time is playing on a flat surface, mastering his or her body movement and control; it's not only tummy time.

- Naps will be twenty to sixty minutes at a time and will happen four to six times a day.
- Total feeding will need to be at least 28 oz. with formula at 20 cal/oz. (the normal formula on the shelf). The most accurate way to get your baby's daily caloric needs will be
  - weight × 55 = calories needed
- The feeds will range 2–4 oz. Do not expect your baby to eat the exact same amount at each feed; what's most important is the total ounces within a twenty-four-hour period.
- Make sure to keep the four o'clock feed for the first three nights at 2 oz. and then pull it completely. Always start your day with a full feed at six o'clock.
- With Transitions One to Three, you are building up to differentiating the day versus the night, learning many skills along the way. Your baby doesn't know what time it is at night, so the feeds prior to this point are monitored by you, but it can be confusing. When baby wakes, he or she is not sure if it's time to eat or time to soothe; all of this is being told to him or her through your body language and communication.
- Our biggest goal for this transition is to keep your baby comforted at any wake and to use milk as a very last resort. With that being said, if milk is needed around four in the morning, only offer two ounces to top your baby off, but don't go for a full feed. This will help for one to two more hours of sleep until your baby is ready to wake and start his or her day with a full feed at six o'clock.
- Think of the four o'clock feed as a "top off" feed. You will be giving this feed to your baby in a very sleepy state, and you will be offering the smaller feed to limit the calories consumed at night and reserving them all for the days.

- Count your daily totals to make sure your baby is staying on track. The exact time of each is less relevant than the grand total for the twenty-four-hour period.
  - Total naps: two and a half to four hours
  - Total floor time: four to six hours
  - Total food: weight × 55 = calories needed
    - To get ounces from this, you will take calories needed and divide by 22 for breast milk and 20–24 for formula, depending on the formula being used.
    - An example would be
      - 15 lb. × 55 = 825 cal
      - 825 cal / 22 cal/oz. = 37.5 oz.
      - An amount of 28–37.5 oz. is what your baby needs per twenty-four hours.
      - Keep in mind some babies will take more or less. It is more important that they follow their growth chart with steady weight gain.

TRANSITION FOUR: SLEEPING THROUGH THE NIGHT

This stretch follows the same plan of the Baby Created Sleep method as the previous transitions. This stretch will occur when your baby weighs at least fifteen pounds and is naturally leaning toward a longer stretch at night. Your baby will show signs of this by occasionally sleeping for longer periods in the night without waking for milk. It will feel like a spontaneous occurrence and usually only happens one night out of the week, but this is your signal. Again, this method is baby created, so just be prepared to follow your baby's readiness for a longer stretch at night.

To help your baby into this stretch, use the same push technique you used for the first transitions. If you are starting with this transition, go through the checklist presented a few pages back to ensure readiness and begin as follows.

When your baby wakes within the first eight hours from bedtime (give or take), don't feed. Instead, soothe your baby back to sleep. In order for this to work, your baby *has* to go back to sleep with the soothing and not with milk. You will spend the duration of the night with your baby to ensure you are quick to respond to a wake and provide a very high level of support. Your baby will wake at times before the four o'clock feed and look to you for a guidance. With your body language and entire aura, you will be communicating to your baby that you are there for soothing and support and that he or she is not alone. At the four o'clock feed, you now offer two ounces, and then you will pull them. This is a longer transition than all previous ones.

This transition will separate your day from night and will be your baby's aha moment. He or she now knows that when he or she sees you in the night, you are there to cuddle and support him or her but not to feed, which allows your baby's digestive system to rest. At Transition Four, he or she finally has hard lines of entering the sleep space and leaving the sleep space as signals for when he or she eats versus when he or she sleeps.

This by no means guarantees you will not be seeing your baby from eight in the evening until six in the morning. It does mean you have established a great communication with each other of what the night is versus day, how he or she can depend on you at night for help, and how you can support him or her through every new journey he or she encounters with patience and love. With this transition, it is extremely important that you focus on your baby's daytime caloric intake. You are now at the point where the calories must be replaced in order to maintain healthy growth and development and will make a big difference if they aren't.

The tools you are working on with your baby are to create happy and healthy associations that will support his or her development of sleep and growth.

You are creating the following associations:

- Establishing a bedtime, which lets your baby and his or her body know when to go into a deeper, more restful, and repairing sleep.

- Establishing morning time, which is the association your baby will have to the end of night and beginning of a day full of activity, learning, and fun.
- Establishing soothing, with the pulling of milk but full support with other soothing techniques. You are showing your baby that he or she is being supported by his or her parents. Milk is a source of nutrients to the body—a requirement of survival. It is also very comforting and soothing to any human. But there are other options for the same love, support, and comfort that are important to find for your child.
- Establishing a full night's sleep, which gives your baby's metabolism and digestive system a break and allows his or her systems to rest and repair throughout the night.

Here is a step-by-step resource for you to use for your transition to a full night's sleep! Transition Four is similar to each of the previous transitions; however, look out for pulling the last feed. You will first reduce the feed to 2 oz. and then pull it altogether. You can use the night-by-night schedule to help with planning a good time to pull the final feed.

- Night one
  - Calculate the daytime for total calories, total floor time, and total number of hours of naps.
  - Bring milk (water/formula) to be made in the nursery in case you need it, but the plan is to not use it until the designated feeding time.
  - If breastfeeding, you will not need to bring milk but need to make your breast inaccessible and not plan on a breastfeeding session.
  - Try an assortment of soothing techniques to get the baby to go back to sleep without milk until four o'clock.
  - Once it is four o'clock, you feed only two ounces (three ounces if your baby is really struggling) and then resume feedings as scheduled (six o'clock).

- At four o'clock, you will offer a 2 oz. feed. This must be offered with a bottle so that you can measure the amount your little one is consuming at this feed. You can't go past four in the morning because it will affect your daytime schedule. This may result in you waking your baby to feed or offering it to him or her while sleeping.
- Once it is morning (six o'clock), *leave* your sleep space (nursery, parents' room, etc.), and start your day schedule.
- It is so very important you soothe your baby back to sleep and then when he or she wakes go for the feed.

- Night two
  - Calculate the daytime for total calories, total floor time, and total number of hours of naps.
  - Bring milk (water/formula) to be made in the nursery in case you need it, but the plan is to not use it until the designated feeding time.
  - If breastfeeding, you will not need to bring milk but need to make your breast inaccessible and not plan on a breastfeeding session.
  - Try an assortment of soothing techniques to get the baby to go back to sleep without milk until four o'clock.
  - Once it is four o'clock, you feed only two ounces (three ounces if your baby is really struggling) and then resume feedings as scheduled (6:00 a.m.).
  - At four o'clock, you will offer a 2 oz. feed. This must be offered with a bottle so that you can measure the amount your little one is consuming at this feed. You can't go past four o'clock because it will affect your daytime schedule. This may result in you waking your baby to feed, or offering it to him or her in his or her sleep.

- Once it is morning (six o'clock), *leave* your sleep space (nursery, parents' room, etc.), and start your day schedule.
- It is very important you soothe your baby back to sleep and then when he or she wakes, go for the feed.
- Nights two and three are typically the most difficult nights and require extensive soothing.

  The most important thing to remember with pushing a feed and soothing is that you get your baby back to sleep without food. If you soothe for twenty-five minutes and get tired and this results in feeding your baby, you will create a very negative association to food and crying for your baby. Instead, stay calm and focus on the support you are giving your baby to get back to sleep.

- Night three
  - Calculate the daytime for total calories, total floor time, and total number of hours of naps.
  - Bring milk (water/formula) to be made in the nursery in case you need it, but the plan is to not use it until the designated feeding time.
  - If breastfeeding, you will not need to bring milk but need to make your breast inaccessible and not plan on a breastfeeding session.
  - Try an assortment of soothing techniques to get the baby to go back to sleep without milk until four o'clock.
  - By night three you will no longer offer any milk, only soothing and support.
  - Once it is morning (six o'clock), *leave* your sleep space (nursery, parents' room, etc.), and start your day schedule.
  - Nights two and three are typically the most difficult nights and require extensive soothing.

The most important thing to remember with pushing a feed and soothing is that you get your baby back to sleep without food. If you soothe for twenty-five minutes and get tired and this results in feeding your baby, you will create a very negative association to food and crying for your baby.

- Nights four and five
  - Calculate the daytime for total calories, total floor time, and total number of hours of naps.
  - Soothe as needed.
  - Once it is morning (six o'clock), *leave* your nursery, and start your day schedule.

To maintain this progress, you must stick with your daytime schedule and forms of soothing at night as needed. The first five nights are the toughest nights over the next three weeks. It is normal to have one to two nights of the week when you have an earlier wake and will need to soothe before the four o'clock feeding.

Now that you have conquered sleeping through the night, relax and enjoy your little one because, as I'm sure you know by now, they grow so quickly. The best way to support nighttime sleep will be meeting your baby's daily needs and ensuring consistency.

Consider the following points to help solidify your sleep training:

1. Keep a full night's sleep. This sounds simple enough, but there is a two- to three-week transition period. Your first five nights of accomplishing this transition are the nights you have a set plan and are focused on calories. The following first week, you will have a few nights (one to three) out of your seven-night week that you have night wake before the morning, so make sure you soothe and keep all of your schedule in place. The third week will show even better results, and the night that you have an early wake, make sure you keep supporting your baby.

2. If your baby has had a low caloric intake for the day, it is vital he or she makes up the calories at night; they can't be lost for proper growth.
   a. This would look like the following:
      i. ✓ Total floor time: at least six hours
      ii. ✓ Total naps: three hours
      iii. ✓ Total ounces: 28 oz. (when typically, your baby has been taking 32 oz.)
      iv. You can see that your day was great, excluding the total amount of milk. On a night like this, you will support your baby until the eight-hour mark, and knowing the calories were low, you might have to feed after that. Once you have gotten past eight hours and your baby wakes up, you will respond with a feed and leaving the nursery. This would be a time you need to go for a feed and make sure you still wake your baby up at six o'clock to start the day. It is important to make up for any lost calories to maintain healthy growth and development. Focus on your calories throughout the day to make sure you get higher numbers for today.
3. Floor time will need to increase to at least six hours a day.
4. Keep in mind a growth spurt is common around four months and again at six months, and these will require more calories and sleep for five to seven days. Your baby will maintain this increase in calories and daily total intake with now be higher.
5. Naps are not yet consolidated, so for now, keep strong with the small catnaps, and don't fret that your baby only sleeps twenty to thirty minutes at a time. It is normal. The total sleep is what matters most.
6. It is mentioned in this transition to do a "top-off feed" at the four o'clock feed of two ounces. It may also be referred to as a "dream feed." Be very careful to keep this in the morning. If you try doing this at, let's say, midnight to try to push the nights longer and

"sneak" in a few extra calories, you are running a very high risk of confusing and triggering the metabolism. Your baby will then be up every two hours expecting a feed.

7. Your baby is the only one who can tell you when he or she is ready to move forward, so read his or her cues, and follow your instincts.

8. You can still follow your nights with cuddles and loves in the family bed. You may even doze in and out of sleep; just make sure you don't fall completely back to sleep for another one to two hours, as this will take away from your naps during the day and set you up for a difficult day.

TROUBLESHOOTING

1. Is your baby very restless and fidgety during sleep?
    a. This can be a sign of too little floor time during the day, in which case you can up your floor time the following day and see quick results.

2. Is your baby showing signs of hunger shortly after a feed?
    a. This can be a sign of low calories per ounce in the milk.
        i. For breast milk, you will need to increase the fat intake in your diet and look for a thick layer of fat separation on the top after being in the refrigerator for thirty-four hours. Ideally this layer should be so thick that when you tilt the bottle from side to side, there is resistance, and the layer is solid across the entire top.
        ii. For formula, you will need to look at the calories per ounce in the nutrition facts on the back of the container. You will want it to be at least 20 cal/oz.

3. Is your baby waking up at two o'clock and is wide awake laughing, smiling, and seemingly ready to start the day?
    a. This is often a sign of too many daytime hours of sleep being taken up and not reserving enough for nighttime.

4. Is your baby starting to roll over?

    a. If your baby is not yet barrel rolling, don't try to unswaddle. This milestone is a great way for your baby to master his or her body movement and choose his or her own sleep position. An alternative option while your baby is still mastering rolling would be to double swaddle. You will only be double swaddling until baby can move freely. You want your baby to be so efficient that he or she can roll in his or her sleep... literally.

CASE STUDY FOUR

Kaidence is hitting so many new milestones and showing such big strides in her development. She was born at forty-one weeks at 6 lb., 7 oz. She was exclusively breastfed for the first few months and is now on formula, as her mother needed to be on a new medication. She has transitioned well through the first three transitions of sleep support, but her parents wanted to wait for the final transition while she switched to her new milk. This is usually a ten-day to two-week process. Kaidence is also rolling over, and they will be pulling the swaddle at the same time.

With pulling the swaddle, it's best to offer daytime naps unswaddled to allow Kaidence time to practice sleeping fully independently and master her skills before doing it throughout the night. Her parents start with naps and allow for all of her naps to be unswaddled for an entire week. They then track all of Kaidence's activity, sleep, and feeds to ensure her readiness for a full night without milk.

On night one, Mom goes and sleeps in the nursery with Kaidence, and any time Kaidence wakes, she is there immediately to soothe and support her until her feed at four o'clock. The feed is now only two ounces and is used just as a top off until the morning.

On nights two and three, Kaidence seems to be more difficult to soothe but is no longer looking for milk. She doesn't take the milk on night three but does want to be held and rocked more. On night four, instead of lifting Kaidence out of the crib, Mom rubs her back, sings to her, and rubs or pats her body in the crib as she moves around to find a good position to sleep in.

By night five, Mom only holds Kaidence's hand through the crib slates and hums when she needs support. On night six, Kaidence sleeps through the night, and by night seven, Mom goes back to her bed. For the next few weeks, there are periodic night wakes, and Mom will go into the room and lay her hand on Kaidence to soothe her and let her know she is there.

SIX MONTHS

SIX MONTHS: STARTING SOLIDS

GIGGLING, SMILING, TALKING, rolling…might as well be walking. Time seems to fly by at this age! Your baby is growing at the speed of light, and here we are again at a huge milestone—starting solids. This is not only a fun time for you and your baby, but it is a milestone that helps in your baby's growth and development. No, it doesn't magically make your baby sleep, but yes, increasing calories will help. We will go over what's normal for this age calorically with great foods to work on, as well as ideas for practicing body movement for what they are capable of developmentally and, of course, for support in getting your little one to sleep longer at night.

Developmentally, your baby has come to quite an advanced place. His or her body is working on overdrive to keep up with the mastering of his or her fine motor skills, bringing toys to his or her mouths, biting on toes, and figuring out his or her limits just to try and push them.

DEVELOPMENTAL PROGRESSION

At six months, your baby should do the following:

- Begin to recognize someone as being a stranger
- Enjoy playing with others (especially his or her parents)
- Respond to other people's emotions
- Enjoy looking in a mirror
- Respond to sound not only by looking but also by making sound himself or herself

- String different vowels together when babbling and enjoy talking to parents
- Respond to his or her own name
- Make sounds that express happiness or displeasure
- Begin to use consonant sounds such as *m*'s and *b*'s
- Continue to look around at nearby things
- Show lots of curiosity about things and attempt to reach things that have previously been out of reach
- Start to pass things from hand to hand
- Roll over in both directions from front to back
- Start to be able to sit without support
- Start to try to support weight on leg(s) when feet are on the floor and may bounce
- Crawl backward before moving forward—sometimes

Here are some red flags to be aware of at the six-month mark:

- Baby doesn't reach and try to grab things that are near him or her.
- Baby doesn't show any affection for known caregivers.
- Baby isn't responding well to sounds around him or her.
- Baby has a hard time bringing things to his or her mouth.
- Baby isn't making vowel sounds.
- Baby isn't able to roll over in either direction.
- Baby doesn't laugh or make noises such as squealing.
- Baby seems to be stiff or have tight muscles.
- Baby seems overly floppy and has little control of movements.

A couple of fun activities to try:

1. Stack blocks and knock them over.
2. Hide-and-seek of any sort—this helps with object permanence and is very important for the separation anxiety around eight to ten months, which is your next step of development.

    a. I also like to practice this by singing to the baby while walking out of his or her line of vision. The baby can still hear you, but he or she cannot see you. This will also help with object permanence.

3. Anything sensory—allow your baby to touch everything, feeling different textures and exploring different materials.

    a. Touch: putting your baby's hands in a bucket filled with uncooked beans, wiggling fingers, and playing.

    b. Sight: books that have both colors and textures are a great resource for connecting hand-eye coordination.

    c. Smell: going outside and smelling pretty flowers in the garden or even the foods while you cook.

    d. Hearing: listening to music and dancing at the same time is great for working on your baby's senses while also working on his or her body movement.

    e. Taste: no matter what style of feeding you choose, allow your little one to taste something that you're eating by licking it, sucking on it, and chewing on it when he or she is ready.

INTRODUCING SOLIDS

Milk is still the primary source for meeting the caloric needs of the baby. Solids come second to support this caloric increase.

Time to get your grub on; if you have started to notice your little one watching every bite you take with envy and curiosity, then you know it's time for food. Your baby should also be sitting independently and have mastered the pincer reflex, where he or she sees something of interest and can bring it to his or her mouth to try it out.

The first thing to note about introducing solids is the myth that having a baby eat cereal helps a baby sleep longer and better. This is false and can actually be dangerous for the baby as it can cause an upset stomach, diarrhea, and an imbalance in the baby's pH. This is because a baby doesn't usually develop the ability to digest the enzymes in grains until around one year old (Michaelis 2016). *So, when introducing solid foods at six months, it is best to begin with fruits and vegetables.*

Solid foods are introduced because of an increased need for calories in a baby that breast milk and formula can no longer keep up with. At six months, a baby's caloric need increases from 500 calories a day to a minimum of 650 calories a day. Because of this, when you are introducing solid foods, it is important to only give the child foods that are high in calories, protein, and fats.

At six months, the baby is still learning how to eat solid foods, so the little food they do consume needs to be rich in nutrients so the baby can get the most out of it. It is also only for play at first, like learning anything new, it takes time to master. From six months to nine months, your baby will be practicing foods, trying to figure out different flavors, textures, and consistency, and during this time you will want to give your baby many options.

A few foods you might consider are the following:

- Avocados
- Pears
- Bananas
- Sweet potatoes
- Bone-in broth-based soup (Bone in because the nutrients will then release out of the bone and into the liquid, which the baby will then consume.)

Babies tend to prefer sweet-tasting items, so it is okay to mix sweet-tasting food with non-sweet-tasting food. For example, you can mix a pear and avocado together.

It is better to give a baby food as a whole instead of pureed. For example, instead of mashing up an avocado, simply cut it into slices, and let the baby handle it himself or herself. Babies have an extremely shallow gag reflex, and this helps not to trigger it. It is a great idea to give a baby an apple (although these aren't high in calories) to practice food with. If you do this, make sure to leave a "handle" on the apple (i.e., leave some skin on the apple, especially if cut into slices) so that the baby finds it easier to hold. Apples are great tools to use to teach a baby how to handle his or her food and about texture, flavor, and the manipulation of food. If you put the apple in the refrigerator beforehand to let it cool, it can be used as a great tool for teething babies. I love using *The Baby-Led Weaning Cookbook* by Gill Rapley and Tracey Murkett as a resource for great recipes and ideas for feeding your growing eater.

	Breast Milk	Formula
After 6 months, baby needs 650 calories	Approximately 100 calories from solid food, and 25 oz. of breast milk	Approximately 100 calories from solid food and 27.5 oz. of formula

It is common to have a baby eating 32–36 oz. a day of milk and only tasting and playing with solids at this point.

When going through a big milestone like adding in solids, you will want to pay close attention to the digestive system and tolerance of the new foods. Signs of concern would be hives around the mouth and chest (really, any hives). It is normal for the skin to get irritated with food and constant drooling, so redness is not a sign of intolerance to the food and could likely result with a rash around the mouth or in the diaper.

With changes in the digestive tract, poops will change either with diarrhea or constipation or an increase in gassiness. If your baby has a difficult time with a certain food during this period, stop it for now but try again within the next month or two. If allergies run high in the family, erring on the side of caution will be beneficial when introducing food to your baby. I like to do a cheek test. This is rubbing food on the outside of the baby's cheek for thirty seconds and then wiping it away and seeing if there is any sort of external reaction.

Make sure your baby is ready for sleep training by using the following checklist. It is important that all boxes be marked prior to beginning any sleep support.

☐ My baby is at least fifteen pounds.

☐ My baby is *not* sick.

☐ My baby has not had a vaccination within the last forty-eight hours.

When weight is less of a concern, you will focus your sleep support on creating a good routine, healthy associations, and supporting the baby where he or she is at. If you have checked all of the items above, then you are ready to start Baby Created Sleep. At fifteen pounds and up, your baby can go one ten-hour stretch in a twenty-four-hour period without a feed. Here is an outline of a schedule that you can follow to ensure enough calories are being consumed, as well as a good starting point for a schedule if you do not already have one in place that works well for your family.

SCHEDULE

At this age, weight should not be much of a concern. So, use the following schedule as a flexible outline that focuses on your morning and bedtime routine and keeping track of your daily totals. If your little one is struggling with weight gain, refer to Transitions Three and Four. These detailed schedules for twelve- to fifteen-pound babies will help ensure healthy sleep support with steady weight gain.

6:30 a.m. feed (4 oz.): Start your day. Morning time will be when you leave the nursery. You can cuddle in the family bed or just start your day with a diaper change, clothes change, conversation, and stimulation. Just leaving the nursery is enough of an environment change to know it's not nighttime anymore.

Total feeds: seven to nine total feeds for daytime of 32–36 oz. (this would be without solids). With solids, aim for three to five times a day for 15–20 oz.

Solid feeds: try three to five times a day. Try a solid food (avocado, banana, sweet potato). At this age, your baby should be eating nutrient-dense, high-protein, and high-fat food to aid in muscle repair and growth as well as brain activity.

Total naps: two to three naps a day, totaling two to three hours. At this time, your baby will consolidate his or her naps into two big naps (forty-five minutes to two hours) and one power nap per day (twenty to forty-five minutes).

Floor time: needs to be at least six hours a day. If your baby is not getting this, it will greatly affect his or her nighttime sleep, causing restlessness.

Family-style dinner: this is important to teach food etiquette and different styles of food.

Power nap: it *can't* be in the crib. This is to ensure a later bedtime and to reset the nervous system and should be no longer than thirty minutes.

6:30–8:30 p.m. feed (2–4 oz.): Close to bedtime doing cluster feeds is the best way to build up calories for nighttime.

8:30 p.m. feed (4 oz.): Bedtime. Here you will have the exact same bedtime and an easily repeatable routine. This routine should be between thirty and forty-five minutes and should be completed in entirety in the sleep space. Ideally, it should not be paired with a bath as this is often stimulating for a lot of babies. It can also create too long a bedtime routine. The bedtime feed will be in the nursery, helping to create a calm and relaxing transition into nighttime sleep.

We need to focus on calories in the daytime to pull them out of the nighttime.

NIGHT PLAN

Soothe all wakes that happen before three o'clock with any type of soothing. You can rock, hold, sing, and so forth; the only thing that you can't do is leave the nursery, turn on any lights, or feed. The most important part of this soothing time is that they fall back to sleep. Remember you are teaching sleep, so keep your eyes closed, stay calm, and keep your body relaxed.

For the first three nights, between three and four o'clock, feed with a three-ounce bottle.

Nights four to ten will consist of soothing, supporting, and patience but no milk.

By six o'clock, begin your day with leaving the nursery and a full feed. If your baby is sleeping, you may have to wake him or her up.

KEY POINTS

Floor activity will be ideally multiple times throughout the day. For the most part, you will only have your baby off the floor if he or she is sleeping. It is considered floor time when you baby is playing on a flat surface, mastering his or her body movement and control; it's not only tummy time.

- Naps will be consolidated at this age, so you have fewer but longer ones, usually one to two hours at a time; they will happen two to three times a day. If your baby sleeps too much during the day, it will take off hours of sleep from the night. You can track his or her total sleep in twenty-four hours for three to five days and get an idea of what the magic number is. It is usually between eleven and fourteen total hours. We reserve nine to ten hours for night and typically two to three for the day.
- Total feeding will need to be at least 28 oz. with formula at 20 cal/oz. (the normal formula on the shelf). The most accurate way to get your baby's daily caloric needs will be
  - weight × 55 = calories needed
- Count your daily totals to make sure your baby is staying on track. The exact time of each is less relevant than the grand total for the twenty-four-hour period.
  - Total nap: two to three hours

- Total floor time: at least six hours
- Total food: weight × 55 = calories needed
  - To get ounces from this, you will take calories needed and divide by 22 for breast milk and 20–24 for formula, depending on the formula being used.
  - An example would be
    - 15 lb. × 55 = 825 cal
    - 825 cal / 22 cal/oz. = 37.5 oz.
    - An amount of 28–37.5 oz. is what your baby needs per twenty-four hours.
    - Keep in mind some babies will take more or less. It is more important that they follow their growth chart with steady weight gain.

You are creating these associations:

- Establishing a bedtime, which lets your baby and his or her body know when to go into a deeper, more restful, and repairing sleep.
- Establishing morning time, which is the association your baby will have with the end of night and the beginning of a day full of activity, learning, and fun.
- Establishing other methods of soothing to create the same love, support, and comfort that milk can provide. You, as the parent, are the source of your baby's support throughout the night. You do not want him or her to cry and then get milk, creating a negative association that the baby has to "work" for his or her milk.
- Establishing a full night's sleep, which gives your baby's metabolism and digestive system a break and allows sleep-wake homeostasis throughout the night, going through full sleep cycles.

If your baby is just getting to 15 lb. and this is your first time stretching out nighttime sleep, you have three options for sleep support.

- The first option is to go through Transitions One to Four, allowing three to five nights each with three days in between to solidify you baby's readiness before moving to the next step (please refer to previous sections for details on each transition).
  - This is most appropriate for babies who have had struggles with weight gain, severe acid reflux, being premature, or dietary intolerances. You will need to make sure your baby does not lose weight by pulling any nighttime feeds.
- The second option is to structure your bedtime and put into place Transition Two, pushing for no feeds for six hours. You will give five nights to get through this transition. Do a one-week break and then push to Transition Four with a 3 oz. feed at four o'clock for seven to ten nights, and follow the transition below.
  - This would be most appropriate for babies with slight issues with weight gain and who possibly have a harder time with transition milk, or for Mom who has a difficult time with supply. Again, it is important your little one does not lose weight. You want to make sure that both Mom and baby have ample time to transition night feeds to the daytime without losing supply or weight.
- The third option is to a seven- to ten-day plan described in the night-by-night transition below. This entails structuring your bedtime and going straight to Transition Four, which is described below.
  - This is most appropriate for your great eaters! Typically, it's for babies who have had no issues with weight gain and will do great with getting enough calories during the day without the nighttime feeds.

Your focus for nights one to three is to fully support your little one while pulling milk from the nighttime. This will likely result with very hands-on soothing such as rocking, holding, and cuddling. You want to make sure this process is being done in a very nurturing and developmentally appropriate way. This is a confusing time for your baby. He or she is used to waking up and getting milk and now is only getting feeds during the day and cuddles from you at night. Through this confusion, it is important to teach your baby to sleep through clear communication. Teaching your little one to sleep will include keeping the room dark and your eyes closed, no talking or acting sleepy (which you probably are), and staying calm.

- Night one
  - Calculate the daytime for calories and total number of hours of naps.
  - Bring milk in case you need it, but the plan is to not use it until the designated feeding time. Try an assortment of soothing techniques to get the baby to go back to sleep without the feed.
  - Once it is four o'clock, you will offer a reduced feed (only 2–3 oz.). This must be offered with a bottle so that you can measure the amount the little one is consuming at this feed. You can't go past four o'clock because it will affect the daytime schedule. This may result in you waking the baby for a feed.
  - Once it is morning (six o'clock), *leave* the nursery, and start the daytime schedule. This is ideally done by the parents to create a stronger association with the day just like the bedtime routine.
  - Plan on rooming in with your baby *and* staying through the night.

- Night two
  - Calculate the daytime for calories and total number of hours of naps.

- Bring milk in case you need it, but the plan is to not use it until the designated feeding time. Try an assortment of soothing techniques to get the baby to go back to sleep without the feed.
- Nights two and three are typically the most difficult nights and require extensive soothing. The most important thing to remember with pushing a feed and soothing is that you get the baby back to sleep without food. If you soothe for twenty-five minutes and get tired and this results in feeding, you will create a very negative association to food and crying for the baby.
- Once it is four o'clock, you will offer a reduced feed (only 2–3 oz.). This must be offered with a bottle so that you can measure the amount the little one is consuming at this feed. You can't go past four o'clock because it will affect the daytime schedule. This may result in you waking the baby for a feed.
- Once it is morning (six o'clock), *leave* the nursery, and start the daytime schedule. This is ideally done by the parents to create a stronger association with the day just like the bedtime routine.
- Plan on rooming in with your baby *and* staying through the night.

- Night three
  - Calculate the daytime for calories and total number of hours of naps.
  - No night feed tonight, so soothing is a must.
    - If you've had a really hard time with pulling milk, you can repeat night two with one feed of 2–3 oz. between three and four o'clock.
  - Nights two and three are typically the most difficult nights and require extensive soothing. The most important thing to remember with pushing a feed and soothing is that you

88

get the baby back to sleep without food. If you soothe for twenty-five minutes and get tired and this results in feeding, you will create a very negative association to food and crying for the baby.

- Once it is morning (six o'clock), *leave* the nursery, and start the daytime schedule. This is ideally done by the parents to create a stronger association with the day just like the bedtime routine.
- Plan on rooming in with your baby *and* staying through the night.

For nights four to six, you will be focusing less on calories and more on figuring out the most efficient form of soothing for your baby. Instead of rocking, soothing, and holding, you can just use your hands in your baby's sleep space to help find positions that are more comfortable and letting your baby know you are there. For example, rolling your baby onto his or her side, with one hand on his or her chest and the other rubbing his or her back or patting his or her bottom, your baby falls into a nice, comfortable sleep knowing you were there with him or her the entire time. Your baby may not have mastered all of his or her motor skills just yet, which can result in erratic movements with limbs waking him or her. Just the support and pressure from your hand, providing a secure touch, can help soothe your baby back to sleep.

- Nights four to six
  - Calculate the daytime for calories and total number of hours of naps.
  - Soothe as needed. Your main focus for these nights is pulling back on how much you soothe.
  - Put a lot of attention on the first wake of the night as it will set your precedence for the entire night. Try to soothe without picking up the baby out of bed.
  - Once it is morning (six o'clock), *leave* the nursery, and start the daytime schedule. This is ideally done by the parents to

create a stronger association with the day just like the bedtime routine.

- Plan on rooming in with your baby *and* staying through the night.

The goal for the final three nights is to provide your baby with the tools he or she needs to support nighttime sleep. At this time, the wakes are usually very infrequent, and you would be going in just when your baby needs you. By now, your baby tool belt should be filled with excellent resources to help your little one at night. As your baby continues to learn sleep and master control over his or her body movements, he or she will begin to rely on you less and less at night. By providing your baby with enough calories during the day, floor time to master motor skills, structured routines, and appropriate hours of total sleep, you've provided him or her the tools needed to master nighttime sleep too.

- Nights seven to ten
  - Calculate the daytime for calories and total number of hours of naps.
  - Soothe as needed, ideally very little, and you have to be a ninja now. You can't be seen at all when going in and out of the room.
  - Stay outside of the room; only go in if needed for light soothing. Be very careful not to let any light in the room as you enter.

TIPS TO HELP SOLIDIFY SLEEP TIME

Now that you have conquered sleeping through the night, relax and enjoy your little one and how quickly he or she is coming along. The way to best support nighttime sleep will be meeting your baby's daily needs, and consistency is always key.

1. Keep a full night's sleep. This sounds simple enough, but there is a two- to three-week transition period to solidify the training. Your

first five nights of accomplishing this transition are the nights you have a set plan and are focused on calories. The following first week, you will have a few nights (one to three) out of your seven-night week that you have night wake before the morning, so make sure you soothe and keep all of your schedule in place. The third week will show even better results, and the night that you have an early wake, make sure you keep supporting your baby.

2. Floor time will need to increase to at least six hours a day, and your baby is cognitively much more advanced, so feeding his or her curiosity and playing is important.

3. Naps are going to either help night sleep or pull away from it. Make sure you follow sleep cues.

4. Your baby is the only one who can tell you when he or she is ready to move forward, so read his or her cues, and follow your instincts.

TROUBLESHOOTING

1. Is your baby very restless and fidgety during sleep?
   a. This can be a sign of too little floor time during the day, in which case you can up your floor time the following day and see quick results.
2. Is your baby showing signs of hunger shortly after a feed?
   a. This can be a sign of low calories per ounce in the milk.
      i. For breast milk, you will need to increase the fat intake in your diet and look for a thick layer of fat separation on the top after being in the refrigerator for thirty-four hours. Ideally this layer should be so thick that when you tilt the bottle from side to side, there is resistance, and the layer is solid across the entire top.
      ii. For formula, you will need to look at the calories per ounce in the nutrition facts on the back of the container. You will want it to be at least 20 cal/oz.

3. Is your baby waking up at two and is wide awake laughing, smiling, and seemingly ready to start the day?
    a. This is often a sign of too many daytime hours of sleep being taken up and not reserving enough for nighttime.
4. Is your baby starting to roll over?
    a. If your baby is not yet barrel rolling, don't try to unswaddle. This milestone is a great way for your baby to master his or her body movement and choose his or her own sleep position. An alternative option while your baby is still mastering rolling would be to double-swaddle. You will only be double swaddling until baby can move freely. You want him or her to be so efficient that he or she can roll in his or her sleep...literally.

SOLIDS TO TRY

Here are some food options for feeding your baby at six to nine months.

Avocado: a quarter cup will provide fifty-five calories, and this is best served whole. Simply slice the avocado in half, leaving the seed in on one side to preserve freshness. Then give the other half to your infant, and let him or her control the amount he or she eats.

Banana: one full banana is 105 calories, and this can be served either full, giving your baby the chance to grip it in his or her hand; in a puree form, which you will smash with a fork and serve as-is or in combination with another item.

Chicken broth: start with peeled carrots, celery, chicken thighs (bone in) or a full bone-in chicken, an onion, and any herb you prefer. I typically add dill and salt to taste. Add all ingredients into a large pot, and bring to a boil for twenty minutes. This needs to cook one to one and a half hours on simmer until chicken in fully cooked and nutrients have been able to leach from the bone. When storing, it is best to separate your ingredients from the broth. Your broth will last up to ten days in the refrigerator, and the other ingredients can be used within five to seven days.

Sweet potatoes: one small potato is 112 calories. Add one sweet potato with the skin on into a pot of water, and allow boiling for forty to fifty minutes or until you can spear with a fork into the potato with ease. Then peel and serve with butter or coconut oil for taste. This is best served warm and in a puree form.

Liver and onions: serve one tablespoon at a time. This is very high in iron and vitamin A. Sauté your onion in butter until brown. Boil the liver in water, and allow cooking through. When you combine them, you need to smash the liver with a fork and mix in the onions in a pan over low heat and season with oil, salt, and pepper to taste.

CASE STUDY FIVE

Baby Elijah has slept with his parents from day one and has always done very well. At this point, his parents feel Eli is ready to sleep in his own bed, and they are ready to start Baby Created Sleep. Eli has been exclusively breastfed and has met all of his milestones for weight gain and development. He is now very mobile, and it has become harder for the family to sleep together. They would like the first transition to be in a crib right next to their bed and then move to Eli's nursery. For now, sleeping next to the bed in a crib is the plan. With beginning solids this month, they will have tried avocados and bananas for the past ten days. Eli loves his food and has had no problem with starting solids.

Now it's time to track daytime intake, total sleep, and floor time for the next two days to make sure we get the totals we need to push the nights. Eli is showing that he needs thirteen and a half total hours of sleep, thirty-two ounces of milk, solids three times a day to play and practice, and floor time has to be all day. He is a very active boy and can no longer be swaddled as he rolls all over the place. So tonight is the night. Eli is going to start with the bedtime routine that he has been doing with his parents at eight o'clock and go to sleep in his crib. He has been taking a nap in his crib once a day for over a week to start getting used to the space as a sleep space.

On the first night, he wakes up after three hours, and Dad soothes him by patting his bottom, and when that no longer works, he picks him up and rocks him in his arms until he falls back to sleep. He woke again at two, and Dad is able to soothe easily with a quick pat on the bottom and humming. When Eli wakes up one hour later, they know he is hungry and go for the three-ounce feed. He starts his day at six thirty, and they focus on high calories all day to help with the night stretch for night two.

It is normal for night two to be tougher than night one, so today Eli had lots of floor time and played outside for some wearing out. Tonight Dad sleeps in the bed next to the crib, so when Eli wakes, he can slip his hand in the crib and touch him for quick soothing, and this works great for the first wake, but by one in the morning, Eli is standing in his crib and upset. Dad rocks him in his arms until he falls to sleep, and this takes longer then it has before. He sleeps until three thirty, and they feed a three-ounce bottle. Mom pushes feeds and tries for even more milk today, and Eli seems to be extrahungry all day.

On night three, Eli woke up only one time and went back to bed with Dad holding his hand through the crib slat. He then started his day at six and ate great. For the next few weeks, there were nights here and there that Eli wakes up, and he is often soothed by a gentle touch or hand holding, but overall he is very easy to get back down. On the nights he wakes up and needs to be held, Mom can hold him and makes note to feed him more the next day. At this point, they see a very direct correlation to a day Eli doesn't eat much and his inability to sleep at night.

EIGHT TO TWELVE MONTHS

SEPARATION ANXIETY/COMMUNICATION

BETWEEN EIGHT AND ten months is when you will notice your little one struggling with separation anxiety. For sleep training at this age, you will focus less on nutrition and more on the communication.

Developmentally you will see your little one physically mastering his or her body and control on a daily basis, which is fun and terrifying at the same time. If you haven't yet, it's time to babyproof the house and the sleep space. Check your crib/basinet for weight limits, and make sure you adjust the height setting to the lowest for your standing babies.

DEVELOPMENTAL PROGRESSION

At nine months, your baby should do the following:

- Show possible fear of strangers
- Be clingy or very attached to specific adults he or she recognizes
- Have toys that are his or her favorites
- Understand the meaning of the word "no"
- Make a lot of different sounds and be able to almost say "Mama" and "Dada"
- Copy sounds and gestures of those around him or her with regularity
- Use fingers to point at things
- Be able to watch something as it falls

- Start looking for things that he or she sees you hide (i.e., know that it's still there)
- Play peekaboo
- Put objects into his or her mouth
- Be able to move objects without any trouble from one hand to the other
- Be able to pick up small objects (such as individual pieces of cereal) between his or her thumb and index finger
- Be able to stand while holding onto something without trouble
- Be able to get into a sitting position on his or her own
- Be able to sit without support
- Use his or her arms to pull himself or herself up to stand
- Be able to crawl

Red flags to be aware of at the nine-month mark:

- Baby isn't able to bear his or her own weight on his or her legs.
- Baby cannot sit up without help.
- Baby doesn't babble or make noises such as "Mama," "Dada," and so forth.
- Baby doesn't play any sort of back-and-forth games.
- Baby isn't responding to his or her own name.
- Baby doesn't recognize people who are often around him or her.
- Baby doesn't look to where you point.
- Baby isn't able to easily transfer objects from one hand to the other.

If the baby is having trouble with any of these things at this stage, it is important to have the parents contact their pediatrician.

A couple of fun things to try:

1. Stack blocks and knock them over.
2. Hide-and-seek of any sort: this helps with object permanence and also helps with separation anxiety.

    a.   I also like to practice this by singing to the baby while walking out of the line of vision while he or she can still hear you singing.

3. Anything sensory: allow your baby to touch everything, feeling different textures and exploring different materials.

    a.   Touch: mix starch with water. If you push on it fast, there will be hard resistance; if you let your hand sink, it will be soft and gooey. This is great for your little one to experience more than one texture.

    b.   Sight: books that have both colors and textures are a great resource for connecting hand-eye coordination. Starting to play with crayons, chalk, and paint is also great for hand-eye coordination.

    c.   Smell: going outside and smelling pretty flowers in the garden or even the foods while you cook.

    d.   Hearing: listening to music and dancing at the same time is great for working on your baby's senses while also working on his or her body movement.

    e.   Taste: no matter what style of feeding you choose, allow your little one to taste something that you're eating by licking it, sucking on it, and chewing on it when he or she is ready. At this age, everything goes to the baby's mouth first as taste is the strongest sense.

4. Sign language: this will give your baby a voice and clear up some miscommunications. It's amazing how much a baby can do at such a young age. Easy ones to start with are "more," "eat," "milk," and "up"!

INTRODUCING A LOVEY

It is often helpful for babies to have an item they can go to for comfort. A lovey is great for this age as it can be the constant throughout any change during the day as well as helping with separation anxiety.

Your baby can be comforted by his or her lovey even if you aren't in the room. You can bring it on a walk, in the car, travelling, to different sleep spaces, and to different care providers. It can also be a support for the parents with soothing when milk is being transferred into the daytime and out of the nighttime.

A lovey is especially helpful for a family who uses its frequent flier miles. If travelling is a big part of your lifestyle, a lovey can be a great tool to ease the transitions from being home to being away.

How to introduce a lovey

A lovey is going to be a big part of your baby's everyday life and always part of his or her soothing. Every time you are comforting your baby, the lovey will be part of the process. Whenever you're feeding, you will bring the lovey and your baby's hand and rub the lovey while they are eating, making it part of the process. Every time your baby falls down and gets a bonk, you grab the lovey and hold the two of them together. It should transfer with your baby everywhere he or she goes, with any new spaces, stroller, car seat, and sleep space when age appropriate.

Nutrition: iron needs to be part of the daily intake now and calories take another large leap. Babies can get iron from meat, liver and onions, leafy greens, and in fortified chew crackers as well. A baby should have mastered solids at this time.

When going through a big milestone like adding in solids, you will want to pay close attention to the digestive system and tolerance of the new foods. Also when weight is less of a concern, you will focus your sleep support on creating a good routine, healthy associations, and supporting the baby where he or she is at.

	Breast Milk	Formula
After 9 months, baby needs 900 calories	Approximately 200 calories from solid food, and 27-28 oz. of breast milk	Approximately 200 calories from solid food and 30 oz. of formula

It is more common to have a baby eating 32–36 oz. a day of milk and eating well.

Here is a checklist to see if your little one is ready for sleep training. Please use this list as a guide to help support you while starting this new transition.

Make sure your baby is ready for sleep training:

- ☐ My baby is at least fifteen pounds.
- ☐ My baby is *not* sick.
- ☐ My baby has not had a vaccination within the last forty-eight hours.

When weight is less of a concern, you will focus your sleep support on creating a good routine, healthy associations, and strong communication with your little one. If you have checked all of these items, then you are ready to start Baby Created Sleep. At fifteen pounds, your baby can go one ten-hour stretch in a twenty-four-hour period.

SCHEDULE

At this age, weight should not be much of a concern. So use the following schedule as a flexible outline that focuses on your morning and bedtime routine and keeping track of your daily totals. If your little one is struggling with weight gain, please refer to Transitions Three and Four. These detailed schedules for twelve- and fifteen-pound babies will help ensure healthy sleep support with steady weight gain.

6:30 a.m. feed (4 oz.): Start your day. Morning time will be when you leave the nursery. You can cuddle in the family bed or just start your day with a diaper change, clothes change, conversation, and stimulation. Just leaving the nursery is enough of an environment change to know it's not nighttime anymore

Total Feeds: seven to nine total feeds for daytime at 32–36 oz. (this would be without solids). With solids, aim for three to five times a day for 25 oz.

Solid feeds: try three to five times a day. Try a solid food (avocado, banana, sweet potato, soups, or sandwiches). At this age, your baby should be eating nutrient-dense, high-protein, and high-fat food to aid in muscle repair and growth as well as brain development. Now that your baby is more comfortable eating solids, it's a good time to introduce more complex, textured foods into his or her diet.

Total naps: two to three naps a day, totaling two to three hours. At this time, your baby will consolidate his or her naps into two big naps (forty-five minutes to two hours) and, if he or she still needs it, one power nap per day (twenty to forty-five minutes).

Floor time: this needs to be at least six hours a day. If your baby is not getting this, it will greatly affect his or her nighttime sleep, causing restlessness.

Power nap: this can't be in the crib. This is to ensure a later bedtime and to reset the nervous system and should be no longer than thirty minutes.

Family-style dinner: this is important to teach food etiquette and different styles of food.

6:30–8:30 p.m. feed (2–4 oz.): Close to bedtime doing cluster feeds is the best way to build up calories for nighttime.

8:30 p.m. feed (4 oz.): Bedtime. Here you will have the same bedtime routine, and the feeds will be in the nursery, helping create a calm and relaxing transition into the nighttime. A bedtime routine should be the exact same every night and easy to repeat. I prefer going into the nursery, changing pajamas and diaper, and feeding milk. While drinking milk, baby will listen to you read a book and sing a song. Then lights out, and put your baby to bed asleep.

NIGHT PLAN

Soothe any wake before three o'clock with any type of soothing. You can rock, hold, sing, and so forth; the only thing that you can't do is leave the nursery, turn on any lights, or feed. The most important part of this soothing time is that your baby falls back to sleep. Remember, you are teaching sleep, so keep your eyes closed, stay calm, and keep your body relaxed.

For the first three nights, between three and four, feed with a three-ounce bottle.

Nights four to ten will consist of soothing, supporting, and patience but no milk.

By six o'clock, begin your day with leaving the nursery and a full feed. If your baby is sleeping, you may have to wake him up.

KEY POINTS

- Communication is the biggest factor at this age. Throughout the day, you can let your little one know what to expect during the nighttime. You can practice communication by saying, "We are going to go eat lunch," and then go eat lunch so that your baby knows when you say something, you will then do it. This helps him or her to understand what you are saying.

- It is developmentally appropriate that your little one be going through a separation-anxiety phase. The best way to support this is clear communication, a lovey, and practicing object permanence.

- Ideally, floor activity will be multiple times throughout the day. You will only have your baby off the floor if he or she is sleeping. Floor time is playing on a flat surface, mastering his or her body movement and control; it's not only tummy time.

- Naps will be consolidated at this age, so you have fewer, but they are longer, usually one to two hours at a time, and will happen two to three times a day. If your baby sleeps too much during the day, it will take hours of sleep from the night. You can track your baby's total sleep in twenty-four hours for three to five days and get an ideal of his or her magic number. It is usually between eleven and fourteen total hours. We reserve nine to ten hours for night and typically two to three for the day.

- Not all babies are the same. Some will already begin to consolidate their naps into one. Don't worry if this happens; you're still looking at your baby's total amount of sleep in a twenty-four-hour period.
- Total ounces will need to be at least 32 oz. with formula at 20 cal/oz. (the normal formula on the shelf). The most accurate way to get your baby's daily caloric needs will be
  - weight × 55 = calories needed
- Count your daily totals to make sure your baby is staying on track. The exact time of each is less relevant than the grand total for the twenty-four-hour period.
  - Total naps: two to three hours
  - Total floor time: at least six hours
  - Total food: weight × 55 = calories needed
    - To get ounces from this, you will take calories needed and divide by 22 for breast milk and 20–24 for formula, depending on the formula being used.
    - An example would be
      - 18 lb. × 55 = 990 calories
      - These calories will be consumed as both milk and solids.

You are creating these associations:

- Establishing a bedtime, which lets your baby and his or her body know when to go into a deeper, more restful, and repairing sleep.
- Establishing morning time, which is the association your baby will have to the end of night and beginning of a day full of activity, learning, and fun.
- Establishing soothing, with the pulling of milk but full support with other soothing techniques. You are showing your baby that he or she is being supported by his or her parents. Milk is a source of nutrients to the body—a requirement of survival. It is

also very comforting and soothing to any human. But there are other options for the same love, support, and comfort that are important to find for your child.

- Establishing a full night's sleep, which gives your baby's metabolism and digestive system a break and allows sleep-wake homeostasis throughout the night, going through full sleep cycles.

Communication: your baby understands what you are telling him or her—truly understands. He or she may not have the words to communicate back to you, but your baby will try with body language or sign language. This is vital to respect your baby's cognitive abilities at this age. When you plan on doing something new, tell your baby. You will often be carrying both sides of the conversation, but they are listening. During the day, you will want to tell your baby the changes that will be happening that night, as well as how you will be supporting him or her through the process. Some examples might be "When you see Mama tonight, you're only going to get love and snuggles but no milk," or "We are only going to have milk during the day. Nighttime is for sleeping."

Separation anxiety is defined as anxiety provoked in a young child by separation or the threat of separation from his or her mother/parent. A child's unwillingness to leave you is a healthy sign of attachment that has developed between the two of you (Separation Anxiety). Ways to help this is to practice, be calm, and consistent, and follow through on promises made. This is only temporary and will resolve quicker when supported and practiced (Separation Anxiety).

If your baby is just getting to 15 lb. and this is your first time stretching out nighttime sleep, you have three options for sleep support.

- The first option is to go through Transitions One to Four, allowing three to five nights each with three days in between to solidify your baby's readiness before moving to the next step (please refer to previous sections for details on each transition).
  - This is most appropriate for babies who have had struggles with weight gain, severe acid reflux, being premature, or

dietary intolerances. You will need to make sure your baby does not lose weight by pulling any nighttime feeds.

- The second option is to structure your bedtime and put into place Transition Two, pushing for no feeds for six hours. You will have five nights to get through this transition, do a one-week break, and then push to Transition Four with a 3 oz. feed at four o'clock for seven to ten nights, and then follow the transition below.
  - This would be most appropriate for babies with slight issues with weight gain and a harder time with transition milk, or for moms who have a difficult time with supply. Again, it is important your little one does not lose weight. You want to make sure that both Mom and baby have ample time to transition night feeds to the daytime without losing supply or weight.
- The third option is to do a seven- to ten-day plan described below in the night-by-night transition. This entails structuring your bedtime and going straight to Transition Four.
  - This is most appropriate for your great eaters! Typically, this is for babies who have had no issues with weight gain and will do great with getting enough calories during the day without the nighttime feeds.

Your focus for nights one to three is to fully support your little one while pulling milk from nighttime. This will likely result with very hands-on soothing such as rocking, holding, and cuddling. You want to make sure this process is being done in a very nurturing and developmentally appropriate way. This is a confusing time for your baby. He or she is used to waking up and getting milk and now is only getting feeds during the day and cuddles from you at night. Through this confusion, it is important to teach your baby sleep through clear communication. Teaching your little one to sleep will include keeping the room dark and your eyes closed, no talking or acting sleepy (which you probably are), and staying calm.

- Night one
  - Calculate the daytime for calories and total number of hours of naps.
  - Bring milk in case you need it, but the plan is to not use it until the designated feeding time. Try an assortment of soothing techniques to get the baby to go back to sleep without the feed.
  - Once it is four o'clock, you will offer a reduced feed (only 2–3 oz.). This must be offered with a bottle so that you can measure the amount the little one is consuming at this feed. You can't go past four o'clock because it will affect the daytime schedule. This may result in you waking the baby for a feed.
  - Once it is morning (six o'clock), *leave* the nursery, and start the daytime schedule. This is ideally done by the parents to create a stronger association with the day just like the bedtime routine.
  - Plan on rooming in with your baby *and* staying through the night.

- Night two
  - Calculate the daytime for calories and total number of hours of naps.
  - Bring milk in case you need it, but the plan is to not use it until the designated feeding time. Try an assortment of soothing techniques to get the baby to go back to sleep without the feed.
  - Nights two and three are typically the most difficult nights and require extensive soothing. The most important thing to remember with pushing a feed and soothing is that you get the baby back to sleep without food. If you soothe for twenty-five minutes and get tired and this results in feeding, you will create a very negative association to food and crying for the baby.
  - Once it is four o'clock, you will offer a reduced feed (only 2–3 oz.). This must be offered with a bottle so that you can

measure the amount the little one is consuming at this feed. You can't go past four o'clock because it will affect the daytime schedule. This may result in you waking the baby for a feed.

- Once it is morning (six o'clock), *leave* the nursery, and start the daytime schedule. This is ideally done by the parents to create a stronger association with the day just like the bedtime routine.
- Plan on rooming in with your baby *and* staying through the night.

- Night three
  - Calculate the daytime for calories and total number of hours of naps.
  - No night feed tonight, so soothing is a must.
    - If you've had a really hard time with pulling milk, you can repeat night two with one feed of 2–3 oz. between three and four o'clock.
  - Nights two and three are typically the most difficult nights and require extensive soothing. The most important thing to remember with pushing a feed and soothing is that you get the baby back to sleep without food. If you soothe for twenty-five minutes and get tired and this results in feeding, you will create a very negative association to food and crying for the baby.
  - Once it is morning (six o'clock), *leave* the nursery, and start the daytime schedule. This is ideally done by the parents to create a stronger association with the day just like the bedtime routine.
  - Plan on rooming in with your baby *and* staying through the night.

For nights four to six, you will be focusing less on calories and more on figuring out the most efficient form of soothing for your baby. Instead of rocking, soothing, and holding, you can just use your hands in your baby's sleep space to help find positions that are more comfortable and letting him or her know you are there. For example, rolling your baby onto his or her side, with one hand on the chest and the other rubbing the back or patting the bottom, your baby falls into a nice, comfortable sleep, knowing you were there with him or her the entire time. You baby may not have mastered all of his or her motor skills just yet, which can result in erratic movements with his or her limbs waking him or her. Just the support and pressure from your hand, providing a secure touch, can help soothe your baby back to sleep.

- Nights four to six
  - Calculate the daytime for calories and total number of hours of naps.
  - Soothe as needed. Your main focus for these nights is pulling back on how much you soothe.
  - Put a lot of attention on the first wake of the night as it will set your precedence for the entire night. Try to soothe without picking up out of bed.
  - Once it is morning (six o'clock), *leave* the nursery, and start the daytime schedule. This is ideally done by parents to create a stronger association with the day just like the bedtime routine.
  - Plan on rooming in with your baby *and* staying through the night.

The goal for the final three nights is to provide your baby with the tools he or she needs to support nighttime sleep. At this time, the wakes are usually very infrequent, and you would be going in just when your baby needs you. By now, your baby tool belt should be filled with excellent resources to help your little one at night. As he or she continues to learn sleep and master control over his or her body movements, he or she will begin to rely on you less and less at night. By providing your baby with enough calories during the day, floor time to master motor skills, structured routines, strong communications, and appropriate hours of total sleep, you've provided him or her the tools he or she needs to master nighttime sleep.

- Nights seven to ten
  - Calculate the daytime for calories and total number of hours of naps.
  - Soothe as needed, ideally very little, and you have to be a ninja now. You can't be seen at all when going in and out of the room.
  - Stay outside of the room; only go in if needed for light soothing. Be very careful not to let any light in the room as you enter.

TIPS TO HELP KEEP NIGHT SLEEP

Now that you have conquered sleeping through the night, it's time to relax and enjoy your little one and how quickly he or she is coming along. The way to best support nighttime sleep will be meeting your baby's daily needs, and consistency is always key.

1. Keep a full night's sleep. This sounds simple enough, but there is a two- to three-week transition period. Your first five nights of accomplishing this transition are the nights you have a set plan and are focused on calories. The first week following, you will have a few nights (one to three) out of your seven-night week that you have night wake before the morning, so make sure you soothe and keep all of your schedule in place. The third week will show even better results, and the night that you have an early wake, make sure you keep supporting your baby.

2. Keep in mind a growth spurt is common around nine months. You will need to increase your baby's daily calories by 150.

3. Naps are going to either help night sleep or pull away from it. If you have too many daytime hours of naps, it will take away from your nighttime hours available for sleep. Make sure you follow sleep cues versus a strict schedule. At this time, your baby is likely

to be consolidating his or her naps to just one, so it's important to follow his or her cues as to when he or she is ready, and what time this will work for him or her.

TROUBLESHOOTING

1. Bumper pads or not? Is your little one able to move independently even in his or her sleep? If the answer is yes, follow safe-sleep guidelines, and make sure you get a good-fitting bumper pad for your crib. Now you can help protect your little one from bumping his or her head on the slats or getting arms and legs stuck through the slats.
2. Is your baby very restless and fidgety during sleep?
    a. This can be a sign of too little floor time during the day, in which case you can up your floor time the following day and see quick results.
3. Is your baby showing signs of hunger shortly after a feed?
    a. This can be a sign of low calories per ounce in the milk.
        i. For breast milk, you will need to increase the fat intake in your diet and look for a thick layer of fat separation on the top after being in the refrigerator for thirty-four hours. Ideally this layer should be so thick that when you tilt the bottle from side to side, there is resistance, and the layer is solid across the entire top.
        ii. For formula, you will need to look at the calories per ounce in the nutrition facts on the back of the container. You will want it to be at least 20 cal/oz.
4. Is your baby waking up at two o'clock and is wide awake laughing, smiling, and seemingly ready to start the day?
    a. This is often a sign of too many daytime hours of sleep being taken up and not reserving enough for nighttime.

SOLIDS TO TRY

Milk is still the primary source for meeting the caloric needs of the baby. Solids come second to support this calorie increase.

Here are some recipes for feeding your baby at six to nine months, adding more complex textures for more advanced eaters.

Fruit kabob: one cup is the daily requirement. Use any combination of fruits that your baby enjoys—grapes, strawberries, bananas, raspberries, kiwis, peaches, and so forth. Cut up fruit in bite-size pieces, and slide on to a straw for safety.

Egg-salad sandwich: use the bread of your choice, and add eggs mashed with oil or mayo, and then add your choice of any additions such as celery, carrots, or pickles. This is to be given to a baby with very low risk of allergies.

Grilled cheese sandwich: use bread and cheese of your choice with broccoli. Butter both sides of the bread, place on warm skillet, and lay down one piece of cheese. Then cut the top off the broccoli, melting it into the cheese, and top it with the other piece of bread. The melted cheese will disguise the texture and taste of broccoli but is a great way to add in some extra nutrients.

Fruit yogurt: use Greek or high-protein yogurt and fruit of choice. Slice the fruit into bite-size pieces, and place on top of the yogurt. This provides two completely different textures for your baby to maneuver in his or her mouth at the same time.

Avocado: a quarter cup will provide fifty-five calories, and this is best served whole. Simply slice the avocado in half, leaving the seed in on one side to preserve freshness. Then give the other half to your infant, and let him or her control the amount he or she eats.

Banana: one full banana is 105 calories, and this can be served either full, giving your baby the chance to grip it in his or her hand, or in a puree form, which you will smash with a fork and serve as-is or in combination with another item.

Chicken broth: start with peeled carrots, celery, chicken thighs (bone in) or a full bone-in chicken, an onion, and any herb you prefer.

I typically add dill and salt to taste. Add all ingredients into a large pot, and bring to a boil for twenty minutes. This needs to cook one to one and a half hours on simmer until chicken is fully cooked and nutrients have been able to leach from the bone. When storing, it is best to separate your ingredients from the broth. Your broth will last up to ten days in the refrigerator, and the other ingredients can be used within five to seven days.

Sweet potatoes: one small potato is 112 calories. Add one sweet potato with the skin on into a pot of water, and allow boiling for forty to fifty minutes or until you can spear with a fork into the potato with ease. Then peel and serve with butter or coconut oil for taste. This is best served warm and in a puree form.

Liver and onions: serve one tablespoon at a time. This is very high in iron and vitamin A. Sauté your onion in butter until brown. Boil the liver in water, and allow cooking through. When you combine them, you need to smash the liver with a fork and mix in the onions in a pan over low heat and season with oil, salt, and pepper to taste.

CASE STUDY SIX

Maximus was sleeping through the night when he was younger. In the last three weeks, he has gone back to waking up every forty-five minutes to an hour. He seems restless, and Mom tries to give him milk, but nothing seems to be working consistently. Sometimes he eats, and other times he just wants to be held. If nothing else works, Mom brings him to bed with her, but he wakes often. He doesn't seem to be happy in any place he sleeps. With this type of sleep exhaustion, Max's parents decided to put a plan is place with Baby Created Sleep.

They start with communication and letting Max know they were going to be sleeping through the night and making changes to his schedule. For two days, they log all of his activity, sleep, and caloric intake. They also work on playing with Max, focusing on his separation anxiety. One thing they have been working on to prepare for this plan is introducing a lovey and a set bedtime routine at eight o'clock every night. The information they gathered let them know Max is eating enough, and he is very active. His total sleep seems to be around thirteen hours. With this they will put a plan in place to offer a ten-hour night, and that leaves three hours of naps available during the day. They will also be moving Max to his own nursery for nighttime sleep.

On the first night, Max goes to bed at eight o'clock, which was a set bedtime that they had been working on for two weeks prior to starting sleep training, and he sleeps until eleven o'clock. When he wakes up the first time, he is expecting to go to his parents' bed and keeps reaching for the door. He has not stayed in his room through the night, but he has been napping in there since he was born. Mom is staying in the room with Max the entire night and makes sure she is quick to his wakes. He is up often through night one and not fully sure why they aren't leaving the nursery. At six o'clock, they both leave the nursery, and Mom makes a note to tell Max they are now starting their day. He has a great day but is very sleepy. Mom makes sure he doesn't sleep over three hours and plays a lot.

Night two they go into the nursery, and Max is slightly difficult to put to sleep and seems to not want to go into his crib. Mom makes sure to let him know she will be with him all night long and stays in the nursery on her own bed (this can be a blow-up mattress). Max wakes up many times and cries very hard at midnight, so his mom stays very calm and makes sure he is fully supported. Every time she holds him or rocks him, she also grabs his lovey to make sure he has it for soothing. Mom noticed Max bonked his head on the crib in the night as he was searching for his lovey, so she added a safe bumper pad to his bed to prevent him from hitting his head or losing his lovey.

By night three, Mom notices if she puts the lovey near Max when he wakes, he likes to hold it and rub his face on it. By night four, every time Max wakes, Mom gives him his lovey and rolls him to his side, rubbing his back, and he quickly goes back to sleep. By night six, Mom goes back to sleeping in her own room, and any time Max wakes, she quickly goes into his room to help him back to sleep. This is usually just giving him his lovey. She notices Max does much better when he has had a day full of activity, and she lets him know every step of the way. Communication means a lot at this stage, and Max does best when he knows what is going on.

ADDITIONAL CASE STUDIES

CASE STUDY SEVEN: SLEEP TRAINING A FULL-TERM AND HEALTHY BABY

THE FIRST EIGHT WEEKS

JENN GOES INTO labor at forty weeks and has a beautiful seven-pound baby girl. After bringing Joslyn home, Mom notices that baby is gaining around one ounce per day and is averaging a two-pound-a-month weight gain. When Joslyn is one month old, she weights nine pounds. Jenn wonders if this means she can start to sleep train as baby has met the weight-gain mark. Jenn called to get advice from a sleep specialist. However, she is told that even though Joslyn is gaining weight, she is not developmentally ready to begin sleep training. Her baby's circadian rhythms haven't come into play yet (despite the baby's weight), and her baby isn't ready to be separated from Mom for that amount of time. This type of separation at such an early age will cause her baby distress.

By eight weeks, her daughter is now eleven pounds, and Mom takes her in for her checkup. Her pediatrician is thrilled by baby's weight gain, development, and growth, and is likewise pleased to hear that breast-feeding has been successful. The doctor lets Mom know that her baby's development has stayed on track perfectly, and she has a clean bill of health. Finally, the doctor informs Mom that it is okay to begin the first stages of sleep training.

BEGINNING TRANSITION ONE WITH SLEEP TRAINING AND STRUCTURE

Jenn begins to create a plan. The first stage of sleep training is for Mom to create a bedtime routine for her baby. First, she sits down with her partner, and the two of them decide that a 9:00 p.m. to 7:00 a.m. schedule will work best for their family, so they set their baby's bedtime at nine o'clock. They also create a bedtime routine that takes almost exactly forty minutes every single night. This includes a diaper change, a feed, a change into pajamas, and the reading of a short book to start off their baby's circadian rhythms for the night. (They know it can't take longer than forty-five minutes, or this will mess with their baby's circadian rhythms and sleep cycles.)

When Joslyn is ten weeks old and the family has been on this routine for some time, they notice that she is naturally starting to sleep for longer periods of time after going to bed. At first, Joslyn would wake within one and a half to two and a half hours after going to bed. Now, about two weeks in, she is starting to sleep between four and five hours a night after she is laid down for bed, waking somewhere between one and two o'clock each morning for a full feed. They know their baby is telling them that she is ready to move forward as these are cues they have been told to look for when sleep training. So they move to the next step of sleep training: removing the first feed.

Transition Two: removing the first feed
Taking this cue from their baby, they decide to move forward with the removal of the first feed. When Joslyn wakes up for a feed at one fifteen that first night, they soothe her back to sleep instead of feeding her. This isn't easy at first. Mom has to pick her up and walk around the room to calm her down and soothe her back to sleep. She doesn't turn the lights on though as this would have the opposite effect and would rouse her. Eventually Joslyn does go to sleep and doesn't wake up again until three.

Upon this second wake, Mom comes back into the room and feeds her baby. She knows that by this second wake, her baby's metabolism has triggered twice, and it is time for her to give her the food she wants.

Over the next three to five days, her baby continues to wake between one and two o'clock in the morning and is soothed back to sleep, and then wakes again between three and four o'clock and is fed. After five days, their baby's metabolism has adjusted, and she no longer wakes before three. Their baby's new wake time is consistently between three and four o'clock.

Ten days later, Joslyn starts showing signs of being ready to push to the next stage of sleep training. Until their baby starts showing these signs and gains the weight, all Mom and her partner have to do is maintain their current schedule.

When Joslyn gains the extra weight, Mom and her partner notice that she has also become a more efficient eater during the day; she eats more quickly and consumes the calories she needs without a problem. They also notice that she is starting to push herself toward a longer stretch in the night. Joslyn is now waking around three thirty to four o'clock consistently.

TRANSITION THREE: PUSHING THE FEED TIME
Mom and her partner use the same push techniques they used in removing the first round of milk. When Joslyn wakes at 3:50 a.m., they don't feed her. Instead they soothe her back to sleep. Then, when she wakes again at 4:50 a.m., they feed her.

They keep this up for the first three to five days while their baby gets used to it. Soon after, she only wakes around five o'clock. Their baby's new wake time is between four and five. They keep this feed until their baby is between fourteen and fifteen pounds.

TRANSITION FOUR: PULLING THE LAST FEED
The removal of the last feed is both the most difficult but most rewarding for Mom and her partner. When their baby reaches fifteen pounds, they again notice that Joslyn is naturally pushing for a longer stretch because she is not finishing her five o'clock feed. The best way to transition out of the last feed is to reduce it from 4 oz. to 2 oz. and then fully take it away.

Joslyn wakes at 4:55 a.m. for a feed. Instead of soothing her back to sleep, Mom reduces the feed from 4 oz. to 2 oz. for the first two nights. Then, on the third night, Mom removes the feed completely and soothes her baby back to sleep. This requires a lot of soothing at first. Mom thinks about her tool belt with all of her options and is able to eventually soothe Joslyn back to sleep.

On the fourth night, when Joslyn wakes again, Mom does the same thing: no milk and soothes back to sleep. This time it is slightly easier to get Joslyn back to sleep. Then, on the fifth night, when Joslyn wakes slightly later, at five fifteen, Mom is able to soothe her back to sleep while keeping her in her crib; she makes "shushing" sounds and rocks her gently back and forth with her hand while baby lays in the crib, and soon she is asleep. On the sixth night, at around 5:20 a.m., Joslyn wakes, and Mom goes in to soothe and only has to place her hand on her baby and wait until she is calmed and back to sleep.

This entire fourth transition takes between five and seven nights, and by the end of it, Joslyn is sleeping soundly until around seven o'clock. Joslyn occasionally still wakes in the middle of the night. On nights like these, Mom and her partner take turns going in to soothe their daughter back to sleep. These nights don't happen too often, and most of the time their daughter sleeps through the night, waking somewhere between six and seven o'clock. This signals the start of the day, and they take their baby, change her diaper, and then immediately remove her from her sleeping environment before giving her a full morning feed. At this point, they have fully supported Joslyn through learning to sleep through the night.

CASE STUDY EIGHT: UNSWADDLING A BABY WHILE SLEEP TRAINING

Mom has a full-term, healthy, and beautiful baby boy, Lucas. At twelve weeks they begin supporting Lucas through sleeping longer stretches at night without a feed. They follow each of the four transitions. Feedings are removed approximately every two to three weeks, and calories are replaced during the day. Baby is gaining weight and working to develop his motor skills.

By five months, Lucas begins rolling with efficiency. Mom and Dad know that is the time to remove the swaddle.

THE REMOVAL OF THE SWADDLE

When removing the swaddle, Mom rooms in with Lucas and lays her blow-up mattress next to the crib. On the first night, Lucas is unsure of what to do with his hands, so Mom simply slips her hands through the crib slats and places her hand on his chest. On night two, Lucas has a harder time finding comfort with his mother's touch, so she stands and holds his arms down to his sides, mimicking the swaddle and allowing him to fall back into a restful sleep. Mom does this for Lucas for the next three nights and notices that he begins to calm faster and even starts to do it on his own.

Mom and Dad know that they have to keep their own cortisol levels down and stay calm, keeping their breathing slow and steady, while not making any noises other than a slight "shushing." The lights need to be kept off. It is imperative to the process that they do all of this because their baby will follow their cues and will imitate what they are doing. If they aren't calm, they can't hope to calm their baby.

BABY SLEEPING POSITIONS AFTER REMOVAL OF SWADDLE

Because Lucas can safely roll at this point (i.e., he is good at barrel rolling), Mom and her partner know they can let him choose whatever position he wants to sleep in. When they lay Lucas down to sleep, they know to lay him on his back, not his stomach. If he rolls over to his stomach on his own, that is okay. Mom and her partner know that they need to be in tune with Lucas as far as what position he chooses.

CASE STUDY NINE: BABY WHO REGRESSES FROM SLEEPING THROUGH THE NIGHT TO WAKING UP MULTIPLE TIMES A NIGHT

Mom has her baby boy, Henry, at full term. His weight gain is great, and he latches easily and is sleeping through most of the night (eight or so hours) on his own by around three and a half to four months old. When

Henry is around six months old, he starts waking up four to six times a night and won't go back to sleep without being fed. He sits up and refuses to be soothed back to sleep.

TRANSITION ONE: SETTING STRUCTURE AND ENSURING DAYTIME CALORIES
To start this sleep-training plan, she implements a daytime feeding schedule for Henry. She feeds him consistently every two hours, making sure to meet his caloric needs. After implementing this daytime feeding schedule, it becomes routine. Mom then establishes a secure bedtime routine for her baby. She chooses an eight o'clock bedtime, as this is around the time the sun sets, in order to work with her baby's circadian rhythms. She also makes sure that his bedtime routine is consistent, including a full feed and change, and doesn't take any longer than forty-five minutes.

TRANSITION TWO
Since Henry is six months old, and over fifteen pounds, it is best to set a time as your goal for the first feed. They will start with six hours as the plan for the second transition. After this bedtime has been established, Mom and Dad go into the room and do everything they can to soothe him back to sleep. This proves difficult as he is used to getting food when he wakes, but Dad starts with the most interactive form of soothing (picking him up, cradling him, walking him around the dark room, making "shushing" noises, etc.), and eventually, they get Henry back to sleep. Dad gently lays him down, following the specific method of moving his body down with baby's so as not to trigger his Moro reflex. Then he keeps his hands on Henry for a few minutes while he is lying in the crib to increase his sense of security before slowly pulling away and backing quietly out of the room. The goal for this transition is removal of calories and providing the highest level of support as Henry is trying to relearn sleeping at night.

They continue to do this for five nights before his metabolism adjusts to support the process, and he consistently wakes up later in the night. After their baby has adjusted to the change, Mom and her partner progress to removing an additional feed in the night. It gets a bit more complicated here as there are certain rules Mom and Dad must follow.

Transition Three: DOWN TO ONE FEED A NIGHT

Anytime Henry wakes before four o'clock, Mom or Dad will go in and soothe him back to sleep. They notice this is easier when they stay in the room with him, and the soothing takes less time as they are able to get to him quicker. When Henry wakes at four fifteen, Mom gives him a full feed of 4 oz. By night four of this transition, they notice that Henry is no longer finishing the 4 oz. bottle at four o'clock. At this time, both parents feel confident that it is time to move to the final transition.

Transition Four: NO MORE NIGHTTIME FEEDS

For two nights, Mom offers a 2 oz. bottle at four o'clock instead of the full feed. By the third night, she offers no milk but soothes baby back to sleep during any wakes that happen in the night. Mom and Dad initially thought that pulling this last feed would be the most difficult. Instead they've found that Henry understands that when they come in at night, there will be no feeds, only soothing. This makes it easier for Henry to differentiate daytime from nighttime.

Other things to know about this retraining

While retraining their baby, Mom and her partner were made aware of a few things they would need to know to implement the successful sleep retraining of their baby.

1. They need to be as in tune with their baby as possible, syncing their nervous systems and following all baby's cues.
2. It is important for whoever was coming into their baby's room to soothe to be quiet and consistent with soothing techniques and to know that each soothing would likely take some time.
3. It is vital that once sleep training has begun, they follow through. They do not want their baby to become confused, knowing that if they give in at any point once they begin, they could

    a. cause negative food and sleep associations for their baby; and

    b. make it that much harder to complete sleep training the next time they attempt it.

4. They might not see full success until the end of sleep training when they remove milk from the night altogether. This is because they would be allowing their baby to complete all of his sleep cycles without interrupting them by starting the metabolism.

5. It is vital that they transfer all of their baby's calories from the nighttime feeds to the daytime. It is important not to lose any calories in the twenty-four-hour period in order to continue healthy weight gain. Each person has a set requirement of calories that need to be consumed daily, and if your baby is consuming them during the day, then the baby's nights can consist of uninterrupted sleep.

6. Once the soothing techniques have been set and the communication is clear, the baby can fully understand the communication of what is daytime and what is nighttime. Here are the three things that have been taught during this process:

    a. Your baby's body expects calories during the daytime and not at night.

    b. The set bedtime and morning-time routines let your baby know when night begins and when it ends.

    c. Your baby is clearly being communicated to that anytime a parent comes into the room at nighttime, the parent is there for support.

CASE STUDY TEN: THINKING OF SLEEP TRAINING A BABY WHO WAS PREMATURE

Mom has a baby boy, Michael, who is born twelve weeks premature and weighs only three pounds, eight ounces. He is taken to the neonatal intensive care unit (NICU), where the doctors work to make sure he is healthy enough to come home. After eight weeks, Mom is thrilled to bring Michael home. At this time, he weighs eight pounds. Mom is excited to have her son home with her although she is curious about sleep training. She looked into it before he was born and planned to do it. She knows that a typical baby usually begins the process at eight weeks old if he or she weighs eight pounds or more. She wants to make sure that she approaches sleep in the most developmental and safe way for Michael.

CAN BABY SLEEP TRAIN OR NOT?

Although her baby meets the age and weight requirements, he doesn't meet the developmental requirements. She needs to wait until Michael's adjusted age is closer to twelve weeks when the circadian rhythms are fully developed. While her baby is technically eight weeks old, his adjusted age is actually thirty-six weeks gestation. Therefore, he will not be ready to sleep train until he begins to show signs on his own. This is much less dependent on the actual number of weeks versus his abilities and readiness for longer stretches. Michael will need time to adjust to being home and learning to survive outside of Mom's womb and the NICU. He will take gradual steps, gaining more control of his body, growing out of the need for oxygen and medical assistance. It is important for Mom to continuously consult with her support team (pediatrician, dietitian, etc.) through this process.

SLEEP TRAINING A PREEMIE

Michael has come a long way, is thriving, and is showing signs of readiness for longer stretches of sleep at night without a feed. Mom begins to support Michael through sleep, starting with Transition One. She spends five nights working on this first transition and finds that Michael handles this well. She then progresses to Transition Two, which he also does well. She is sure to pay close attention to Michael's daytime caloric intake. By Transition Three, Michael has a harder time with this. Mom decides to stay at this transition until he adjusts and is ready to move forward.

Michael is sleeping comfortably until four o'clock, but when he wakes, he finishes his full bottle, showing signs that he was truly hungry. It takes six weeks before he naturally starts to sleep a little bit longer, at which time Mom moves to the last transition of pulling all the nighttime feeds.

CASE STUDY ELEVEN: SLEEP TRAINING TWINS

Mom gives birth to twin girls, Mia and Ava, at thirty-seven weeks. While they were a few weeks premature, they were born healthy and happy and only had to stay an extra few days at the hospital. When Mom brings them home, she works at bonding with both Mia and Ava, learning who they are, how best to soothe them, and mastering tandem feeding. She makes sure to keep both babies' schedules in sync with each other. All the while, her babies grow, develop, and are consistently gaining weight.

Things to know and focus on before beginning sleep training for twins:

- Fourth trimester: the main goals for Mia and Ava during this time is to gain weight, transition from the womb, bond with parents, and begin developing a schedule that works for all of them.
- Routine: creating a daytime routine keeps the schedules in sync with each other. It is ideal for twins to eat and sleep at the same time and, most importantly, that they are kept together.
- Bonding: as Mom and Dad are building their relationships with Mia and Ava, they have to also remember that the girls depend on each other and need each other.
- Taking turns: follow the lead of the smaller, lower weight twin. This often means the larger twin will need to wait.

THINGS TO BE AWARE OF WHILE SLEEP TRAINING TWINS

Eventually, Mia and Ava are ready to start sleep training, so Mom starts the first few steps (i.e., implementing a daytime schedule first and then a bedtime routine that doesn't take longer than forty-five minutes). After these have been established, Mom takes away the first feed, following the transitions. When the girls wake for their first feeds, she soothes them back to sleep, and when they wake for a second time in the night, she feeds them.

Mom continues with this transfer/pulling of calories technique. When Mia and Ava wake for the second time, and she goes to feed them, only one baby (the smaller twin, Ava) wants to feed. Mia may not take a full feed when the smaller one does, and this is okay because she may be taking larger feeds during the daytime. If Mia doesn't want as much milk, all Mom has to do is simply reduce it down to two ounces (while Ava gets a full feed). This will help her keep their schedules in sync, and they will have their next feed together as a full feed.

Mia and Ava are noisy because they like to talk to each other. So soothing in the nighttime requires a fine-tuned ear as to when they actually need Mom and when they are just talking to each other. Moving to the last transition, Mia sleeps through more easily than Ava does, so Mom focuses her energy on Ava with additional support.

CASE STUDY TWELVE: LOW WEIGHT GAIN IN A BABY AND WHAT IT MEANS FOR SLEEP TRAINING

NOTICING THERE IS A PROBLEM

Mom has a baby girl, Mallory, full term, at six pounds, seven ounces, and she plans to exclusively breastfeed her. Baby latches well, although it does seem to take a decent amount of practice, and there is a distinct learning curve. After about three and a half weeks at home, however, Mom notices that Mallory doesn't weigh what she would have expected by this point. She knows that babies, on average, gain about half a pound a week, and so her baby should be about eight pounds. Mallory has only gained ten ounces in the past three weeks. She knows this is a red flag, and she consults her pediatrician, who tells her that her breast-feeding relationship with her baby likely needs help and support. The doctor tells her to bring her baby in for an appointment and advises her to meet with her lactation consultant about what she can do to change her feeding relationship with her baby.

The next day, the pediatrician confirms that there is nothing wrong with her daughter except that she seems to not be getting all the nutrition she needs. This confirms what he originally stated, that there is likely an issue with the feeding relationship. Mom goes straight to see her lactation consultant to come up with a new feeding plan.

THE NEW FEEDING PLAN

Over the next couple of months, Mom works with her resources to come up with a plan that will get Mallory back on track with appropriate weight gain. This is done over multiple trials and errors, but once they are on track and things have stabilized, they can move forward to starting sleep support once Mallory is old enough and of the proper weight.

WHAT LOW WEIGHT GAIN MEANS FOR SLEEP TRAINING

Mallory is five months and is very active. She is sitting, rolling, and even starting to scoot forward. Typically babies with low weight gain excel with their fine motor skills. Sleep training at this point is less dependent on age and more on weight. The best way to support the progression would be to start with Transitions One and Two and maintain this until Mallory gains the weight she needs to push to Transition Three. This is a better option versus keeping three- to four-hour feeds in the nighttime. It is common that a baby with low weight gain will go four-hour stretches at nighttime. Although this may feel more restful for the parents, it is better to support the sleep development by having a six-hour stretch and then resuming two-hour feeds to help prepare for future sleep support.

To the sleep-deprived parent,

I know that you're tired, and I know that makes this seems like something really hard to undertake. Each of the tools provided in my book will help those final puzzle pieces fall into place. Your tool belt is now full of ways to communicate with your little one and know exactly how to support them.

Trust that by listening to your instincts, counting calories, and through patience, you will reach your goal! Each night that you stay true to this process you will begin to notice a more positive outcome. My biggest piece of advice is to hang in there, it will get better. What seems unachievable now, will soon be a thing of the past. You can do it!

Sincerely,

Rachelle

BIBLIOGRAPHY

Cherry, Kendra. 2015. "What Is the Moro Reflex?" *About Health*. October 30. Accessed April 7, 2016. http://psychology.about.com/od/mindex/g/mororeflex.htm.

Coley, Rachel. 2015. "Tips for Transitioning from Sleeping in Baby Gear to Sleeping Flat." CanDoKiddo. Accessed March 31, 2016. http://www.candokiddo.com/news/baby-sleeping-flat-on-back.

Felicetti, M. 2012 "How to Balance Your pH to Heal Your Body." September 24. Accessed September 1, 2015. http://www.mindbodygreen.com/0-6243/How-to-Balance-Your-pH-to-Heal-Your-Body.html.

HealthyChildren.org. 2012. "A Parent's Guide to Safe Sleep." April. Accessed March 31, 2016. https://www.healthychildren.org/English/ages-stages/baby/sleep/Pages/A-Parents-Guide-to-Safe-Sleep.aspx.

LoveYourBaby.com. 2016. "Baby Pee." Accessed April 6. http://www.loveyourbaby.com/baby-pee.html.

Kangaroo Care. 2015. "Kangaroo Care." June 16. Accessed April 6, 2016. https://my.clevelandclinic.org/childrens-hospital/health-info/ages-stages/baby/hic-Kangaroo-Care.

KidsHealth.org. 2016. "Separation Anxiety." July 25. http://kidshealth.org/en/parents/sep-anxiety.html

Macklin, Ken. 2015. "Newborn Human Babies Can't Shiver; That's Why They Have Brown Fat." *Sciengist*. August 16. Accessed April 6, 2016. http://www.sciengist.com/newborn-human-babies-cant-shiver-thats-why-they-have-brown-fat/.

Mayo Clinic Staff. 2014. "Milk Allergy." August 7. Accessed April 7, 2016. http://www.mayoclinic.org/diseases-conditions/milk-allergy/basics/symptoms/con-20032147.

Michaelis, Kristin. 2016. "Why Ditch the Infant Cereals? | Food Renegade." Accessed April 1, 2016. *Foodrenegade.com.* http://www.foodrenegade.com/why-ditch-infant-cereals/.

Oxford Dictionaries Language Matters. 2016. "Definition of Colostrum in English." Accessed April 6. http://www.oxforddictionaries.com/us/definition/american_english/colostrum?q=Colostrum.

Oxford Dictionaries Language Matters. 2016. "Definition of Sphincter in English." Accessed April 6. http://www.oxforddictionaries.com/us/definition/american_english/sphincter.

Rapley, Gill, and Tracey Murkett. 2010. *Baby-Led Weaning Cookbook: Over 130 Delicious Recipes for the Whole Family to Enjoy.* London: Vermilion.

What to Expect. 2015. "Spotting and Preventing Dehydration in Babies" July 9. Accessed April 6, 2016. http://www.whattoexpect.com/first-year/dehydration-in-babies.

ZERO TO THREE. 2014. "SUPPORT US." Accessed March 10, 2016. http://main.zerotothree.org/site/PageServer?pagename=ter_key_brainFAQ.